FISH

superb ways with seafood

& shellfish

FISH

superb ways with seafood

& shellfish

contributing editor:
LINDA DOESER

HERMES
HOUSE

This edition published by Hermes House
an imprint of
Anness Publishing Limited
Hermes House
88-89 Blackfriars Road
London SE1 8HA

A CIP catalogue record for this book is available
from the British Library

Publisher: Joanna Lorenz
Cookery Editor: Linda Doeser
Copy Editor: Leslie Viney
Designer: Mason Linklater
Illustrator: Madeleine David

Printed and bound in China

Previously published as '*Great Fish & Shellfish*'

© Anness Publishing Limited 1999
Updated © 2003
5 7 9 10 8 6 4

NOTES

Standard spoon and cup measures are level.

Large eggs are used unless otherwise stated.

CONTENTS

Introduction

Often called the "harvest of the sea," fish, shellfish and other seafood offer almost endless possibilities for delicious, nutritious and healthy meals. There are a vast number of different preparations for fish: grilled, baked, steamed, served in a creamy sauce, combined with fruit or vegetables, curried, wrapped in parchment or served cold in salads, to name just a few. The recipes in this book have been inspired by dishes from all over the world and explore interesting ways of cooking both familiar and unfamiliar varieties.

The book begins with an introduction to the main types of fish, with some helpful hints on buying and storing fish and useful equipment. This is followed by a step-by-step guide to techniques, including trimming, gutting, skinning, scaling, preparing steaks and cutlets and filleting. Techniques for seafood follow, with instructions for preparing mussels and clams, opening oysters and scallops and deveining shrimp. This section is completed with a guide to basic cooking techniques: poaching, steaming, grilling, and coating and frying. The recipes themselves are divided into seven chapters: Soups, Appetizers, Salads, Pasta and Rice, Fried and Grilled Dishes, Pies and Baked Dishes, and Casseroles and Stews.

Besides being easy and quick to prepare, seafood is highly nutritious and plays an important role in the modern cook's approach to preparing healthy meals. Modern research confirms the value of fish in the diet for lowering cholesterol levels, as well as offering many other health benefits.

More than anything else, fish—whether freshwater or from the sea—offers immense scope to the creative cook. The recipes here range from the simple yet delicious to the elaborate and self-indulgent. There are recipes to suit all tastes and budgets and dishes suitable for every occasion.

Types of Fish and Seafood

Fish can be almost any size and color and range from the solitary bottom dwellers in the deep ocean to the huge schools of coastal fish. However, from the cook's point of view, they fall into three categories: round fish, flat fish (both sea types) and freshwater fish.

Round fish

This large group, which includes such familiar varieties as herring, cod, haddock, whiting, pollack, anchovy, sprat, sardine, grouper and mullet, are distinguished by having a rounded body, eyes on either side of the head and by swimming with their dorsal (back) fin on top. As well as bony fish, it includes cartilaginous species, such as dogfish and shark. Round fish are usually sold whole, in fillets or in steaks. Many of the oily varieties, such as mackerel and tuna, are delicious grilled or fried. White fish, such as whiting, which has a particularly delicate flavor and fine texture, may be fried or poached. Firm-fleshed fish is ideal for baking or stuffing. Salmon are included in this group, although part of their life cycle is spent in fresh water.

Flat fish

This group, which includes sole (lemon and Dover), plaice, dab, flounder, turbot and halibut, swim on one side and have both eyes on the same side of the head. Usually the lower, blind side is paler than the upper side of the fish. Most flat fish, with the exception of halibut, turbot and skate, is sold whole or in fillets. The very large varieties are usually available as steaks, and only the wings of skate are sold. The shallow bodies of flat fish and their generally firm but tender and flavorful flesh make them ideal for grilling or sautéing.

Freshwater fish

Aside from trout, which nowadays is readily available as a farm fish, these are not so frequently seen as seawater fish. Favorite freshwater fish include bream, perch, St. Peter's fish, char, pike, carp, freshwater catfish and eel.

Crustaceans

This group covers all the aquatic creatures, both fresh- and sea-water, with five pairs of legs: lobster, crab, shrimp, crayfish and crawfish. They tend to have firm, sweet flesh and many have heavy front claws or pincers. The head and body are usually, but not invariably, enclosed in a tough shell or carapace. Shrimp are often sold cooked, although they are also available raw. Crabs and lobsters are fresher and more delicious if they are bought live, but some people find it distressing to kill them. Shrimp are especially delicious gently sautéed, while lobster is particularly suited to delicate poaching.

Shellfish

This group includes single-shelled mollusks, such as the whelk and periwinkle, and the more popular bivalves, such as oysters, mussels, clams and scallops. It also includes the family to which squid, cuttle-fish and octopus belong. Some shellfish, especially oysters, are usually eaten raw in their own juices from the shell. Cockles and razor shells may also be eaten raw, but are good in soups, too. Mussels and clams are delicious steamed in their own juices or in white wine and lemon juice, and scallops are

often poached. All shellfish should be bought on the same day it is going to be eaten as it turns bad extremely quickly.

Buying and storing

When choosing fish, it is the appearance and smell that reflect its condition. When buying whole fish, look for shining skin, bright color, pink gills and full bright eyes with black pupils and trans-

parent corneas. The flesh should be soft but springy, and the body should be firm. Genuinely fresh fish has a clean, pleasant odor, so reject any with even a suggestion of a "fishy smell." The only exceptions are shark and skate. This is because their flesh contains a chemical that breaks down after death to yield ammonia, which has an irritating smell. It is best to store skate and shark for a couple of days after they have been caught before preparing and cooking.

Shellfish deteriorate more rapidly than fish. Many, such as clams and mussels, are sold alive for this reason. Cooked crab, lobster and shrimp are available, and some types of shellfish are sold frozen. However, neither has quite the same flavor and texture as fresh seafood. As a general rule, you can tell if seafood is fresh because it does not smell.

Seafood will stay fresh for no longer than one day if stored in the refrigerator. Wrap it loosely in waxed paper or foil to prevent its smell from penetrating other foods. Fish freezes well, but you should be sure that it really is fresh and has not already been frozen on the fishing ship and thawed before sale.

Equipment

Divided fish lifter
A useful gadget that opens out so that you can lift a whole fish or large fillet of fish with one hand without breaking it.

Filleting knife
A long, flexible knife is essential for skinning and filleting fish, as it can curve around the shape of the body, its bones and flesh. Keep the knife as sharp as possible.

Fish grid for the barbecue
This circular grid is ideal for cooking whole small fish, such as sardines, on the barbecue. Place the fish in the shaped grid and position on the barbecue, turning the whole grid over halfway through the cooking time.

Fish kettle
This elongated saucepan, fitted with a trivet or rack, is used to poach large, whole fish, such as salmon. Place the fish on the trivet with water in the base of the kettle and make sure that the lid is tight fitting. Poach on the stove or in the oven. Kettles are available in different sizes and there is even a specially shaped kettle made for poaching turbot, but this is really not essential equipment for a domestic kitchen.

Fish platter
A large flat platter essential for displaying whole fish. It makes an attractive centerpiece, particularly on a buffet table.

Fish server
Good for lifting fish fillets or single portions of fish.

Fish terrine mold
Ideal for large fish pâtés or terrines. Always cook in a *bain marie*: in other words, placed in a large roasting pan, filled halfway up the side of the terrine mold with boiling water. Cast iron molds are ideal for cooking the terrine, but make sure that they are always covered with the lid and line the mold with waxed paper to make removal easy. Serve the terrine sliced.

Fish-shaped mousse mold
An attractive way to present a cold mousse or fish mold.

Large fish server
Useful for lifting whole fish and large fillets lengthwise.

Oyster knife
A tool made expressly for opening tightly closed oyster shells. You can pry the shells apart with the strong blade.

Scaler
This is perfect for scraping off stubborn scales. Alternatively, you can use a blunt knife. In either case, this is best done under running water.

Skewers
Use to cook brochettes on the barbecue or under the broiler.

Strong scissors
Good for trimming fins and tails.

Whole fish grid for the barbecue
This is designed for cooking a whole large fish on the barbecue. Gut before cooking and season well. Wrap in large sprigs of fresh herbs, such as rosemary. Turn over halfway through the cooking time.

Zester
A quick method to add citrus fruit zest to any stuffing or marinade or to make a quick, fresh garnish.

Trimming Round Fish

1 With a pair of heavy scissors, cut off the fins on either side of the fish, then cut away the ventral or belly fins.

2 Cut off the dorsal fins along the back.

3 Trim the tail by cutting a "V" shape into it.

Gutting Round Fish Through the Stomach

1 With a medium knife, slit the underside of the fish from the gills to the small ventral opening. Take care not to insert the knife too far.

2 Carefully loosen the stomach contents from the cavity with your fingers and pull them out.

3 Using a teaspoon, scrape along the vertebrae in the cavity to remove the kidney.

4 Pull out the gills. Wash the cavity with cold water.

Gutting Round Fish

1 With a heavy pair of scissors, cut along the fish's belly.

2 Remove the insides with your fingers and wash the cavity.

Boning Round Fish for Stuffing

1 Gut the fish through the stomach as described on the previous page.

2 Slit the fish on either side of the backbone, cutting the flesh away from the bone until it is completely detached.

3 With a heavy pair of scissors, snip the backbone once at the head and once at the tail.

4 Carefully lift out the backbone and discard.

Boning a Round Fish Through the Stomach

1 Gut the fish through the stomach as previously described. Continue the stomach slit on one side of the backbone as far as the tail.

2 Open the cavity and remove the insides.

3 Clean the insides of the fish, wiping away any remaining blood or guts.

4 Open the cavity and, with the blade of the knife, cut away the loose inside bones that line the flesh.

5 Turn the fish over and slit the flesh at the base of the backbone on the other side.

6 With the blade of the knife, cut loose the inside bones lining the flesh in the same way as the first side.

7 Carefully loosen the backbone of the fish completely.

8 With scissors, snip the backbone at the head and the tail.

9 Carefully peel the backbone away from the flesh with any inside bones.

10 The head can be kept and the two side fillets rolled in spirals, skin side inward. Alternatively, fold the skin outward and tuck the tail inside.

11 Alternatively, the head and skin can be removed and the fillets rolled or cooked flat.

Cutting Steaks and Cutlets

1 With a large, sharp knife, slice the fish across, at a right angle to the backbone, into slices of the desired thickness.

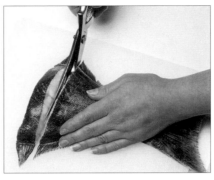

2 If necessary, cut through the backbone with kitchen scissors or a knife with a serrated blade.

Filleting Round Fish

1 Holding the knife horizontally, slit the skin from head to tail along one side of the backbone.

2 Cut down to the backbone just behind the fish's head.

3 Holding the knife flat and keeping the blade in contact with the bone, cut off the flesh from head to tail in a continuous slicing motion.

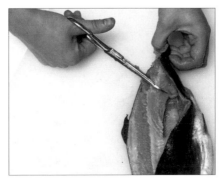

4 Cut the backbone at the tail end with scissors.

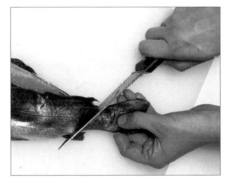

5 Trim off the tail.

6 Cut the fish into two fillets.

Skinning a Fillet

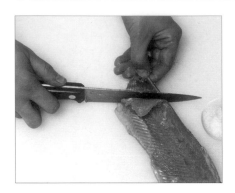

1 Secure the fillet with salt on a cutting board. Insert a sharp, flexible knife at the end of the fillet and hold securely.

2 Working in a cutting motion against the skin, move the knife along the fillet.

3 Continue until the skin has been completely removed from the flesh.

Boning Flat Fish

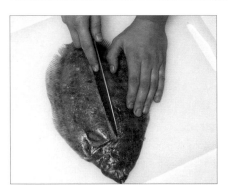

1 Using a flexible knife, cut along the backbone.

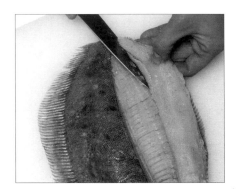

3 Cut to the edge of the transverse bones, but do not remove the fillet completely.

7 Loosen the bones from the flesh of the fish.

2 Cut the flesh away from the bones, holding the knife almost parallel to them.

4 Turn the fish over and repeat for the opposite fillet.

5 Fold both fillets out.

6 Using a strong pair of scissors, cut the bones along the edges.

8 With kitchen scissors, snip the backbone at both the head and the tail ends.

9 Lift the backbone at the tail end and pull, stripping it from the flesh underneath.

Filleting Flat Fish

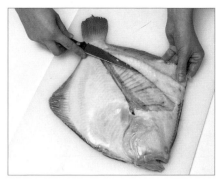

3 Turn the fish over and cut a straight line from the tail to the head as before.

4 Work the flesh away from the bones as described in steps 1 and 2, and then repeat with the fourth fillet.

1 With a sharp knife, cut around the edge of the fish to outline the shape of the fillets. Cut a straight line from the tail to the head along the spine through the bone. Keeping the knife almost flat, slip it between the flesh and the rib bones.

2 Cut away the fillet, using a stroking motion and keeping the knife flat. Continue cutting until the fillet and flesh against the fins has been detached with the skin in one piece. Continue with the other fillet.

Skinning Flat Fish

1 Lay the fish on a cutting board, with the dark side on top. With a sharp knife held at an angle, cut across the skin where the tail joins the body, taking care not to cut all the way through.

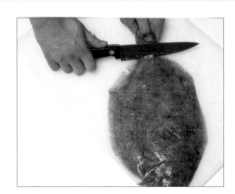

2 With the knife still held at an angle, start to cut. Keep the fish secure on the board with some salt and gradually pry the flap of skin away from the flesh. When you have a good flap of skin, grasp it with one hand and hold the other end of the fish with your other hand. Firmly pull the skin toward the head.

Fish Stock

1½ pounds heads, bones and trimmings
　　from white fish
1 onion, sliced
2 celery stalks with leaves, chopped
1 carrot, sliced
½ lemon, sliced (optional)
1 bay leaf
3–4 fresh parsley sprigs
6 black peppercorns
5½ cups water
½ cup dry white wine

1 Rinse the fish heads, bones and trimmings under cold running water. Put them in a large saucepan with the vegetables, lemon, if using, herbs, peppercorns, water and wine. Bring to a boil, skimming the surface frequently. Reduce the heat and simmer for 25 minutes.

2 Strain the stock, but do not press down on the contents of the strainer. If you are not using the stock immediately, let cool and then refrigerate. Fish stock should be used within 2 days. It may be frozen and kept for up to 3 months.

Preparing Mussels and Clams

Mollusks, such as mussels and clams, should be eaten very fresh and should be alive when you buy and cook them (unless they have been shelled and frozen or are canned). You can tell if they are alive because their shells are tightly closed. Any that are open should shut immediately when tapped sharply with a knife. Any that do not close or that have broken shells should be discarded.

If you have collected the shellfish yourself, let them stand in a bucket of sea water for several hours, changing the water once or twice. Do not use fresh water, as it will kill them. Add one or two handfuls of cornmeal or flour to the water to help clean the stomachs of the shellfish. Shellfish bought from a shop will already have been purged of sand.

1 Scrub the shells with a stiff brush and rinse well. This can be done under cold running water.

2 Pull off the "beards" (their anchor threads) with the help of a small knife. Rinse well.

3 To steam, put a little dry white wine or water in a large saucepan, together with any flavorings specified in the recipe. Add the mussels or clams, cover tightly and bring to a boil. Cook for 5–10 minutes or until the shells open, shaking the pan from time to time. Discard any that do not open.

4 Serve the shellfish in their shells or shell them before using. Strain the cooking liquid, which includes the liquid from the shells, and spoon it over the shellfish or use it as the basis for a seafood sauce.

5 To open a live clam or mussel, hold it in one hand with the hinge in your palm. Insert the side of a clam or oyster knife blade between the shell halves and work it around to cut through the hinge muscle.

6 Open the shell and cut the clam or mussel out of the shell. Do this over a bowl to catch all the liquid from the shell.

Opening and Cleaning Scallops

1 To open the shell, hold the scallop with the flat shell on top. Probe between the shells with a short knife to find a small opening. Insert the blade and run it across the roof of the shell.

2 Separate the two halves of the shell, and pull apart.

3 Slide the blade under the grayish outer rim of the flesh, called the skirt, to free the scallop. Pull off the muscle with a small knife. Use the trimmed scallop, whole or halved, for cooking.

Opening Oysters

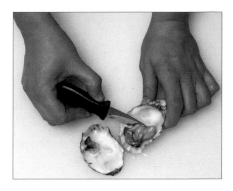

1 Place the oyster, wrapped in a clean napkin or dish towel, on a firm surface with the flatter shell on top and the hinge toward you. Holding the oyster with one hand, insert the tip of an oyster knife into the gap in the hinge.

2 Twist the blade to snap the shells apart.

3 Continue to hold the oyster firmly in the cloth and slide the blade along the inside of the upper shell to sever the muscle that holds the shell together. Discard the top shell and lift the lower, rounded shell off the napkin, making sure the liquid in it does not spill. Clean any bits of broken shell with the point of the knife.

4 Grip the lower shell firmly with your fingers. Cutting toward yourself, run the blade under the oyster to sever the muscle attaching it to the lower shell and free it.

Preparing and Deveining Shrimp

Shrimp may be cooked in their shells, but are often peeled first. The shells can be used to make an aromatic stock. The intestinal vein that runs down the back is usually removed from large shrimp, mainly because of its appearance, but also because it may contain grit that makes it unpleasant to eat. Shrimp may be sold with the heads on. These are easily pulled off with the fingers and will enhance the flavor of stock made with their shells.

1 Holding the shrimp firmly in one hand, pull off the legs with the fingers of the other hand.

2 Peel the shell away from the body. When you reach the tail, hold the body and pull away the tail; the shell will come off with it. Alternatively, you can leave the tail on the shrimp and just remove the body shell.

3 Make a shallow cut down the center of the curved back of the shrimp. Pull out the black vein with a toothpick or your fingers.

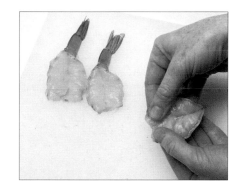

4 To make butterfly shrimp, cut along the deveining slit to split open the shrimp, without cutting all the way through. Open up the shrimp flat.

5 To devein shrimp in their shells, insert a toothpick horizontally in several places along the back where the shell overlaps to lift out the vein.

Poaching

Whole fish, large and small, as well as fillets, cutlets and steaks, are excellent poached because the gentle cooking gives succulent results. Poached fish can be served hot or cold with a wide variety of sauces. The poaching liquid may be used as a basis for the sauce.

1 To oven poach small, whole fish, fillets, cutlets or steaks, place the fish in a buttered, flame-proof dish that is large enough to hold the pieces in a single layer. Pour in enough liquid to come two-thirds of the way up the sides of the fish.

2 Add any flavorings specified in the recipe. Press a piece of buttered waxed paper on top to keep in the moisture.

3 Set the dish over medium heat and bring the liquid just to a boil. Transfer the dish to a pre-heated oven at 350°F and poach until the fish is just cooked. To test, with the tip of a sharp knife, make a small cut into the thickest part of the fish, ideally near a bone. The flesh should be slightly translucent.

4 To poach whole fish, fillets, cutlets or steaks on the stove, put large whole fish on the rack in a fish kettle or set on a piece of muslin that can be used like a hammock. Small whole fish, fillets, cutlets and steaks may be poached in a fish kettle on a rack or set directly in a wide saucepan or frying pan.

5 Prepare the poaching liquid— water, milk, wine or stock—in the fish kettle, a large casserole, a roasting pan, a wide saucepan or frying pan, as appropriate. Set the rack in the kettle or the muslin hammock in the casserole or pan. Add more liquid if necessary.

6 Cover the kettle or casserole and bring the liquid just to a boil. Reduce the heat and simmer very gently until the fish is cooked.

Steaming

This simple, moist-heat method of cooking is ideal for fish and shellfish. If you do not have a steamer, it is easy to improvise.

1 Using a steamer, arrange the fish on the steamer rack and set over boiling water. Cover and steam until done.

2 For Chinese-style steaming, arrange the fish on a heatproof plate that will fit inside a bamboo steamer or wok. Put the plate in the steamer or on the rack in the wok, set over boiling water, cover and steam until done.

3 For steaming larger fish and fillets, arrange the fish on a rack in a roasting pan of boiling water or on a plate set on the rack. Cover tightly with foil and steam until done.

4 To steam in foil, wrap the fish and seasonings in foil, sealing well, and set on a rack in the steamer or in a large roasting pan of boiling water. Steam until done.

Broiling

1 To broil small, whole oily fish, boned and butterflied fish, fillets, cutlets and steaks that are at least ½ inch thick or cubes of fish on skewers, rinse the fish and pat it dry with paper towels. Marinate the fish if the recipe suggests this.

2 Preheat the broiler with the broiler pan in place. When hot, lightly brush the hot pan with oil. Arrange the fish in the pan in a single layer, skin side down, brush the fish with butter, oil or a basting mixture, according to the recipe.

3 Set the fish under the broiler, 3–4 inches from the heat. Thin pieces should be closer to the heat for a shorter time than thicker ones. Broil, basting once or twice and turning if the recipe specifies, until the fish is done.

4 To broil leaner, small whole fish, steaks, cutlets and fillets that are at least ½ inch thick and prepared for cooking as above, arrange in a buttered, flameproof dish. Add a little liquid—wine, stock or court bouillon—just to cover the base of the dish. Brush the fish with butter, oil or a basting mixture, according to the recipe. Broil as above, without turning the fish.

Coating and Frying

1 Lightly beat an egg in a shallow dish. Spread some flour on a plate or sheet of waxed paper and season with salt and freshly ground black pepper or ingredients as specified in the recipe. Spread fine bread crumbs or crushed crackers on another plate or sheet of waxed paper.

2 To egg and crumb large pieces of fish, dip the fish first in the seasoned flour, turning to coat both sides lightly and evenly. Shake or brush off excess flour.

3 Next, dip the floured fish in the egg, turning to moisten both sides.

4 Dip the fish in the crumbs, turning to coat evenly. Press to help the crumbs adhere. Shake or pat off excess crumbs. Chill for at least 20 minutes to set the coating.

5 To egg and crumb small pieces of fish, strips of fish fillet or shrimp, put the crumbs in a plastic bag. After dipping the fish in seasoned flour and egg, toss a few pieces at a time in the plastic bag of crumbs.

6 To pan fry, heat some oil or a mixture of oil and butter in a frying pan, using enough to coat the base of the pan in a thin layer or according to recipe instructions. When it is very hot, put the fish in the pan in a single layer. Fry until golden brown on both sides and the fish is done. Drain on kitchen paper before serving.

7 To deep-fry, half fill a deep pan with oil and heat it to 375°F. Gently lower the coated pieces of fish into the hot oil, frying them only a few at a time. Fry until golden brown, turning them occasionally, so that they cook evenly. Remove and drain thoroughly on paper towels before serving.

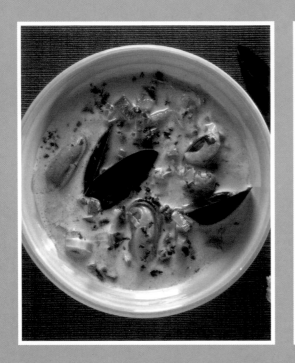

SOUPS

Smoked Haddock and Potato Soup

The traditional name for this soup is "cullen skink." A cullen is the "sea town" or port district of a town, while "skink" means stock or broth.

Serves 6

1 finnan haddock, about 12 ounces

1 onion, chopped

bouquet garni

4 cups water

1¼ pounds potatoes, quartered

2½ cups milk

2 tablespoons butter

salt and freshly ground black pepper

snipped chives, to garnish

1 Put the haddock, onion, bouquet garni and water into a large saucepan and bring to a boil. Skim the scum from the surface, then cover the pan. Reduce the heat and poach for 10–15 minutes, until the haddock flakes easily.

COOK'S TIP

Finnan haddock is a small, whole fish that has been soaked in brine and then cold smoked.

2 Lift the haddock from the pan, using a fish server, and remove the skin and bones. Flake the flesh and reserve. Return the skin and bones to the pan and simmer, uncovered, for 30 minutes.

3 Strain the fish stock and return to the pan, then add the potatoes and simmer for about 25 minutes, or until tender. Remove the potatoes from the pan using a slotted spoon. Add the milk to the pan and bring to a boil.

4 Meanwhile, mash the potatoes with the butter, then whisk into the milk in the pan until thick and creamy. Add the flaked fish to the pan and adjust the seasoning. Sprinkle with chives and serve immediately with crusty bread.

Corn and Scallop Chowder

Fresh ears of corn are ideal for this chowder, although canned or frozen corn also works well. This soup makes a perfect lunch dish.

INGREDIENTS

Serves 4–6

2 ears of corn or 1 cup frozen or
   canned corn

2½ cups milk

1 tablespoon butter or margarine

1 small leek or onion, chopped

1 small garlic clove, crushed

4 strips bacon, finely chopped

1 small green bell pepper, seeded
   and diced

1 celery stalk, chopped

1 medium potato, diced

1 tablespoon flour

1¼ cups chicken or vegetable stock

4 scallops

4 ounces cooked fresh mussels

pinch of paprika

⅔ cup light cream or half-and-half
   (optional)

salt and freshly ground black pepper

1 Using a sharp knife, slice down the ears of the corn to remove the kernels. Place half of the kernels in a food processor or blender and process with a little of the milk.

2 Melt the butter in a large saucepan and gently fry the leek or onion, garlic and bacon for 4–5 minutes, until the leek is soft but not browned. Add the diced green pepper, chopped celery and diced potato and sweat over low heat for another 3–4 minutes, stirring frequently.

3 Stir in the flour and cook for 1–2 minutes, until the mixture is golden and frothy. Gradually stir in the milk and corn mixture, stock, the remaining milk and corn kernels and seasoning.

4 Bring to a boil, then reduce the heat and simmer, partially covered, for 15–20 minutes, until the vegetables are tender.

5 Pull the corals away from the scallops and slice the white flesh into ¼-inch slices. Stir the scallops into the soup, cook for 4 minutes and then stir in the corals, mussels and paprika. Heat through for a few minutes and then stir in the cream, if using. Adjust the seasoning to taste and serve.

Classic Italian Fish Soup

Liguria, Italy, is famous for its fish soups. In this one the fish are cooked in a broth with vegetables and then puréed. This soup can also be used to dress pasta.

INGREDIENTS

Serves 6

2¼ pounds mixed fish or fish pieces, such as whiting, red mullet, pollack or cod

6 tablespoons olive oil, plus extra to serve

1 medium onion, finely chopped

1 stalk celery, chopped

1 carrot, chopped

¼ cup chopped fresh parsley

¾ cup dry white wine

3 medium tomatoes, skinned, seeded and chopped

2 garlic cloves, finely chopped

6 cups boiling water

salt and freshly ground black pepper

rounds of French bread, to serve

1 Scale and clean the fish, discarding all the innards, but leaving the heads on. Cut into large pieces. Rinse well in cool water.

2 Heat the oil in a large saucepan and add the onion. Cook over low to medium heat until it begins to soften. Stir in the celery and carrot, and cook for 5 more minutes. Add the parsley.

3 Pour in the wine, raise the heat, and cook until it reduces by about half. Stir in the tomatoes and garlic. Cook for 3–4 minutes, stirring occasionally. Pour in the boiling water, and bring back to a boil. Cook over medium heat for 15 minutes.

4 Stir in the fish, and simmer for 10–15 minutes or until the fish are tender. Season with salt and pepper.

5 Remove the fish from the soup with a slotted spoon. Discard the heads and any bones. Purée in a food processor. Taste for seasoning. If the soup is too thick, add a little more water.

6 To serve, heat the soup to simmering. Toast the rounds of French bread, and sprinkle with olive oil. Place 2 or 3 in the base of each soup plate before pouring over the soup.

Shellfish with Seasoned Broth

Leave one or two mussels and shrimp in their shells to add an extra touch to this elegant dish.

INGREDIENTS

Serves 4

1½ pounds mussels, scrubbed and
    debearded
1 small fennel bulb, thinly sliced
1 onion, thinly sliced
1 leek, thinly sliced
1 small carrot, cut in julienne strips
1 garlic clove
4 cups water
pinch of curry powder
pinch of saffron
1 bay leaf
1 pound large raw shrimp, peeled
1 pound small shelled scallops
6 ounces cooked lobster meat,
    sliced (optional)
salt and freshly ground black pepper
1–2 tablespoons chopped fresh chervil or
    parsley, to serve

2 Put the fennel, onion, leek, carrot and garlic in a saucepan and add the water, reserved mussel liquid, spices and bay leaf. Bring to a boil, skimming any foam that rises to the surface, then reduce the heat and simmer gently, covered, for 20 minutes, until the vegetables are tender. Remove the garlic clove.

3 Add the shrimp, scallops and lobster meat, if using, then after 1 minute, add the mussels. Simmer gently for about 3 minutes, until the scallops are opaque and all the shellfish are heated through. Adjust the seasoning, then ladle into a heated tureen and sprinkle with the chervil.

1 Put the mussels in a large heavy saucepan or flameproof casserole, cover with water and cook, tightly covered, over high heat for 4–6 minutes, until the shells open, shaking the pan or casserole occasionally. When cool enough to handle, discard any mussels that did not open and remove the rest from their shells. Strain the cooking liquid through a muslin-lined sieve and reserve.

Bouillabaisse

Perhaps the most famous of all Mediterranean fish soups, this recipe, originating from Marseilles in the south of France, is a rich and colorful mixture of fish and shellfish, flavored with tomatoes, saffron, orange and Pernod.

INGREDIENTS

Serves 4–6

3–3½ pounds mixed fish and raw shellfish, such as red mullet, monkfish, red snapper, large raw shrimp and clams

8–10 ripe tomatoes

pinch of saffron strands

6 tablespoons olive oil

1 onion, sliced

1 leek, sliced

1 celery stalk, sliced

2 garlic cloves, crushed

1 bouquet garni

1 strip orange rind

½ teaspoon fennel seeds

1 tablespoon tomato paste

2 teaspoons Pernod

salt and freshly ground black pepper

4–6 thick slices French bread and 3 tablespoons chopped fresh parsley, to serve

1 Remove the heads, tails and fins from the fish and set the fish aside. Put the trimmings in a large pan with 5 cups water. Bring to a boil, and simmer for 15 minutes. Strain into a bowl, and reserve the liquid.

2 Cut the fish into large chunks. Leave the shellfish in their shells. Scald the tomatoes for 20 seconds, then drain and refresh in cold water. Peel and roughly chop them. Soak the saffron in 1–2 tablespoons hot water.

3 Heat the oil in a large pan, add the onion, leek and celery and cook until softened. Add the garlic, bouquet garni, orange rind, fennel seeds and tomatoes, then stir in the saffron and soaking liquid and the fish stock. Season with salt and pepper, then bring to a boil and simmer for 30–40 minutes.

4 Add the shellfish and boil for about 6 minutes. Add the fish and cook for another 6–8 minutes, until it flakes easily.

5 Using a slotted spoon, transfer the fish to a warmed serving platter. Keep the liquid boiling, to allow the oil to emulsify with the broth. Add the tomato paste and Pernod, then check the seasoning. To serve, place a slice of French bread in the base of each soup bowl, pour the broth on top and serve the fish separately, sprinkled with the parsley.

COOK'S TIP

Saffron comes from the orange and red stigmas of a type of crocus. These must be harvested by hand and it requires about 250,000 crocus flowers for a yield of 1¼ pounds of saffron. Consequently, it is extremely expensive—the highest-priced spice in the world. However, its slightly bitter flavor and pleasantly sweet aroma are unique and cannot be replaced by any other spice. It is an essential ingredient in all traditional versions of bouillabaisse and should not be omitted.

Shrimp Bisque

The classic French method for making a bisque requires pushing the shellfish through a tamis, or drum sieve. This is much simpler and the result is just as smooth.

INGREDIENTS

Serves 6–8

1½ pounds small or medium cooked
    shrimp in the shell
1½ tablespoons vegetable oil
2 onions, halved and sliced
1 large carrot, sliced
2 celery stalks, sliced
8 cups water
a few drops of lemon juice
2 tablespoons tomato paste
bouquet garni
2 tablespoons butter
¼ cup flour
3–4 tablespoons brandy
⅔ cup whipping cream
salt and freshly ground white pepper
flat leaf parsley sprig, to garnish

1 Remove the heads and peel off the shells from the shrimp, reserving them for the stock. Chill the shrimp.

2 Heat the oil in a large pan, add the shrimp heads and shells and cook over high heat, stirring frequently, until they start to brown. Reduce the heat to medium, add the onions, carrot and celery and fry gently, stirring occasionally, for about 5 minutes, until the onions start to soften.

3 Add the water, lemon juice, tomato paste and bouquet garni. Bring the stock to a boil, then reduce the heat, cover and simmer gently for 25 minutes. Strain the stock through a sieve.

4 Melt the butter in a heavy saucepan over medium heat. Stir in the flour and cook until just golden, stirring occasionally. Add the brandy and gradually pour in about half of the shrimp stock, whisking vigorously until smooth, then whisk in the remaining liquid. Season to taste. Reduce the heat, cover and simmer for 5 minutes, stirring frequently.

5 Strain the soup into a clean saucepan. Add the cream and a little extra lemon juice to taste, if desired, then stir in most of the reserved shrimp and cook over medium heat until hot. Serve immediately, garnished with the remaining shrimp and parsley.

Mussel Bisque

Served hot, this makes a delicious and very filling soup, perfect for a light lunchtime meal. It is also excellent cold.

INGREDIENTS

Serves 6

1½ pounds fresh mussels in their shells

⅔ cup dry white wine or dry cider

2 cups water

2 tablespoons butter

1 small red onion, chopped

1 small leek, thinly sliced

1 carrot, finely diced

2 tomatoes, skinned, seeded and chopped

2 garlic cloves, crushed

1 tablespoon chopped fresh parsley

1 tablespoon chopped fresh basil

1 celery stalk, finely sliced

½ red bell pepper, seeded and chopped

1 cup whipping cream

salt and freshly ground black pepper

1 Scrub the mussels and pull off the beards. Discard any with broken shells or any that do not close when sharply tapped. Place them in a large pan with half the wine and ⅔ cup of the water.

2 Cover and cook the mussels over high heat until they open up. (Discard any that do not open.) Transfer the mussels with a draining spoon to another dish and set aside until cool enough to handle. Remove the mussels from their shells, leaving a few in their shells to garnish, if desired.

3 Strain the cooking liquid through a clean piece of muslin or a fine cloth to remove any traces of sand or grit. Heat the butter in the same large pan and cook the onion, leek, carrot, tomatoes and garlic over high heat for 2–3 minutes.

4 Reduce the heat and cook for another 2 3 minutes, then add the cooking liquid, remaining water and wine, the parsley and basil and simmer for another 10 minutes. Add the mussels, celery, red pepper, cream and seasoning to taste. Serve hot or cold.

Seafood Soup with Rouille

This is a really chunky, aromatic mixed-fish soup from France, flavored with plenty of saffron and herbs. Rouille, a fiery hot paste, is served separately for everyone to swirl into their soup to flavor.

INGREDIENTS

Serves 6

3 red mullet, scaled and gutted

12 large raw or cooked shrimp

1½ pounds white fish, such as cod, haddock, halibut or monkfish

8 ounces fresh mussels

1 onion, quartered

5 cups water

1 teaspoon saffron strands

1 tablespoon boiling water

5 tablespoons olive oil

1 fennel bulb, roughly chopped

4 garlic cloves, crushed

3 strips orange rind

4 thyme sprigs

1½ pounds tomatoes or 1 can (14 ounces) chopped tomatoes

2 tablespoons sun-dried tomato paste

3 bay leaves

salt and freshly ground black pepper

For the rouille

1 red bell pepper, seeded and chopped

1 red chili, seeded and sliced

2 garlic cloves, chopped

5 tablespoons olive oil

¼ cup fresh bread crumbs

1 To make the rouille, process the pepper, chili, garlic, oil and bread crumbs in a blender or food processor until smooth. Transfer to a serving dish and chill.

2 Fillet the mullet by cutting off the flesh from either side of the backbone, reserving the heads and bones. Cut the fillets into small chunks. Peel half the shrimp and reserve the trimmings to make the stock. Skin the white fish, discarding any bones, and cut the flesh into large chunks. Scrub the mussels well, discarding any damaged ones and any that do not close immediately when tapped sharply with the back of a knife.

3 Put the fish trimmings and shrimp trimmings in a saucepan with the onion and water. Bring to a boil, then simmer gently for 30 minutes. Cool slightly and strain.

4 Soak the saffron in the boiling water. Heat 2 tablespoons of the olive oil in a large sauté pan or saucepan. Add the mullet and white fish and fry over high heat for 1 minute. Drain.

5 Heat the remaining oil and fry the fennel, garlic, orange rind and thyme until beginning to color. Measure the strained stock and add water until you have 5 cups of liquid.

6 If using fresh tomatoes, plunge them into boiling water for 30 seconds, then refresh in cold water. Skin and chop. Add the stock to the pan with the saffron, tomatoes, sun-dried tomato paste and bay leaves. Season to taste. Bring almost to a boil, lower the heat, then simmer gently, covered, for 20 minutes.

7 Stir in the mullet, white fish and shrimp, peeled and unpeeled, and add the mussels. Cover the pan and cook for 3–4 minutes. Discard any mussels that do not open. Serve the soup hot with the rouille.

COOK'S TIP

To save time, order the fish and ask the fishmonger to fillet the mullet for you.

Spiced Mussel Soup

Chunky and colorful, this Turkish fish soup is similar to a chowder in its consistency. It is flavored with harissa sauce, more familiar in North African cooking.

INGREDIENTS

Serves 6

3–3½ pounds fresh mussels

⅔ cup white wine

3 tomatoes

2 tablespoons olive oil

1 onion, finely chopped

2 garlic cloves, crushed

2 celery stalks, thinly sliced

bunch of scallions, thinly sliced

1 potato, diced

1½ teaspoons harissa sauce

3 tablespoons chopped fresh parsley

freshly ground black pepper

thick yogurt, to serve

1 Scrub the mussels and remove the beards, discarding any with damaged shells or any open ones that do not close immediately when tapped sharply with a knife.

2 Bring the wine to a boil in a large saucepan. Add the mussels and cover with a lid. Cook for 4–5 minutes, until the mussels have opened fully. Discard any mussels that remain closed. Drain the mussels, reserving the cooking liquid. Strain the cooking liquid through a clean piece of muslin or fine cloth to remove any traces of grit. Reserve a few of the mussels in their shells for a garnish and shell the remainder.

3 Plunge the tomatoes into boiling water for 30 seconds, then refresh in cold water. Skin and dice them. Heat the olive oil in a heavy pan and fry the onion, garlic, celery and scallions for 5 minutes, until golden.

4 Reserve a little of the onion mix. Add the shelled mussels, reserved liquid, potato, harissa sauce and tomatoes. Bring just to a boil, reduce the heat and cover. Simmer gently for 25 minutes or until the potato is breaking up.

COOK'S TIP

Harissa is a spicy purée made from peppers, cayenne, olive oil, garlic, coriander, cumin and mint.

5 Stir in the parsley and pepper and add the reserved mussels. Heat through for 1 minute. Garnish with the reserved onion mix. Serve hot with a spoonful of yogurt.

Fish and Okra Soup

The inspiration for this soup came from a traditional Ghanaian recipe. Chop the okra to achieve a more authentic consistency.

INGREDIENTS

Serves 4

2 green bananas

4 tablespoons butter or margarine

1 onion, finely chopped

2 tomatoes, skinned and finely chopped

4 ounces okra, trimmed

8 ounces smoked haddock or cod fillet, cut into bite-sized pieces

3¾ cups fish stock

1 fresh chili, seeded and chopped

salt and freshly ground black pepper

chopped fresh parsley, to garnish

3 Add the fish, fish stock, chili and seasoning to the pan. Bring to a boil, then reduce the heat and simmer for about 20 minutes or until the fish is cooked through and flakes easily.

4 Peel the cooked bananas and cut into slices. Stir into the soup, heat through for a few minutes and then ladle into soup bowls. Sprinkle with the chopped parsley and serve.

1 Slit the skins of the green bananas, but do not peel. Place them in a large saucepan. Cover with water, bring to a boil and cook over medium heat for about 25 minutes or until the bananas are tender. Transfer to a plate and let cool.

2 Melt the butter in a large saucepan and sauté the chopped onion for about 5 minutes, until soft. Stir in the chopped tomatoes and okra and fry gently for another 10 minutes.

Noodle Soup with Pork and Szechuan Pickle

This soup is a meal in itself, and the hot pickle gives it a delicious tang.

INGREDIENTS

Serves 4

4 cups chicken stock

12 ounces egg noodles

1 tablespoon dried shrimp, soaked in
   water

2 tablespoons vegetable oil

8 ounces lean pork, finely shredded

1 tablespoon yellow bean paste

1 tablespoon soy sauce

4 ounces Szechuan hot pickle, rinsed,
   drained and shredded

pinch of sugar

2 scallions, finely sliced, to garnish

1 Bring the stock to a boil in a large saucepan. Add the noodles and cook until almost tender. Drain the dried shrimp, rinse them under cold water, drain again and add to the stock. Lower the heat and simmer for another 2 minutes. Keep hot.

2 Heat the oil in a frying pan or wok. Add the pork and stir-fry over high heat for 3 minutes.

3 Add the bean paste and soy sauce to the pork; stir-fry for 1 more minute. Add the hot pickle with a pinch of sugar. Stir-fry for 1 more minute.

4 Divide the noodles and soup among individual serving bowls. Spoon the pork mixture on top, then sprinkle with the scallions and serve immediately.

Snapper and Noodle Soup

Tamarind gives this light, fragrant noodle soup a slightly sour taste.

INGREDIENTS

Serves 4

8 cups water

2¼ pounds red snapper (or other red fish,
   such as mullet)

1 onion, sliced

½ cup tamarind pods

1 tablespoon fish sauce

1 tablespoon sugar

2 tablespoons vegetable oil

2 garlic cloves, finely chopped

2 lemon grass stalks, very finely chopped

4 ripe tomatoes, roughly chopped

2 tablespoons yellow bean paste

8 ounces rice vermicelli, soaked in warm
   water until soft

1 cup bean sprouts

8–10 basil or mint sprigs

¼ cup roasted peanuts, ground

salt and freshly ground black pepper

1 Bring the water to a boil in a saucepan. Lower the heat and add the fish and onion, with ½ teaspoon salt. Simmer gently until the fish is cooked through.

2 Remove the fish from the stock; set aside. Add the tamarind, fish sauce and sugar to the stock. Cook for 5 minutes, then strain into a bowl. Carefully remove all the bones from the fish, keeping the flesh in big pieces.

3 Heat the oil in a large frying pan. Add the garlic and lemon grass and fry for a few seconds. Stir in the tomatoes and bean paste. Cook gently for 5–7 minutes, until the tomatoes are soft. Add the stock, bring back to a simmer and adjust the seasoning.

4 Drain the vermicelli. Plunge it into a saucepan of boiling water for a few minutes, drain and divide among individual serving bowls. Add the bean sprouts, fish and basil or mint and sprinkle the ground peanuts on top. Fill up each bowl with the hot soup.

Crab and Egg Noodle Broth

This delicious broth is the perfect solution when you are hungry, time is short, and you need something fast, nutritious and filling.

INGREDIENTS

Serves 4

4 ounces fine egg noodles

2 tablespoons unsalted butter

1 small bunch scallions, chopped

1 celery stalk, sliced

1 medium carrot, peeled and cut
   into batons

5 cups chicken stock

¼ cup dry sherry

4 ounces white crab meat, fresh or frozen

pinch of celery salt

pinch of cayenne pepper

2 teaspoons lemon juice

1 small bunch cilantro or flat leaf parsley,
   to garnish

3 Add the chicken stock and sherry to the pan, bring to a boil, reduce the heat and simmer for another 5 minutes.

4 If using frozen crab meat, let it thaw. Flake the crab meat between your fingers onto a plate and remove any stray pieces of shell.

5 Drain the noodles and add to the broth, together with the crab meat. Season to taste with celery salt and cayenne pepper and sharpen with the lemon juice. Return to a simmer.

6 Ladle the broth into shallow soup plates, scatter with roughly chopped cilantro to garnish and serve.

1 Bring a large saucepan of water to a boil. Toss in the egg noodles and cook according to the instructions on the package. Cool under cold running water, drain and leave immersed in water until required.

2 Heat the butter in another large pan, add the scallions, celery and carrot, cover and soften the vegetables over low heat for 3–4 minutes.

Corn and Crab Meat Soup

This soup originated in the United States, but it has since been introduced into China. You must use creamed corn in the recipe to achieve the right consistency.

INGREDIENTS

Serves 4

4 ounces crab meat or chicken breast

2 teaspoons finely chopped fresh ginger

2 egg whites

2 tablespoons milk

1 tablespoon cornstarch paste

2½ cups vegetable or chicken stock

1 can (8 ounces) creamed corn

salt and freshly ground black pepper

finely chopped scallions, to garnish

1 Flake the crab meat (or roughly chop the chicken breast) and mix with the ginger.

2 Beat the egg whites until frothy, add the milk and cornstarch paste and beat again until smooth. Blend with the crab meat or chicken breast.

3 In a wok or saucepan, bring the stock to a boil, then add the creamed corn and bring back to a boil.

4 Stir in the crab meat or chicken breast and egg-white mixture, adjust the seasonings to taste and stir gently until well blended and the meat is cooked. Serve garnished with finely chopped scallions.

Main Course Spicy Shrimp and Noodle Soup

This dish is served as a hot coconut broth with a separate platter of shrimp, fish and noodles. Diners are invited to add their own choice of accompaniments to the broth.

INGREDIENTS

Serves 4–6

½ cup shelled, raw cashews

3 shallots, or 1 medium onion, sliced

2-inch piece lemon grass, shredded

2 garlic cloves, crushed

6 ounces spaghetti-size rice noodles, soaked for 10 minutes

2 tablespoons vegetable oil

½-inch square piece shrimp paste, or 1 tablespoon fish sauce

1 tablespoon mild curry paste

1 can (14 ounces) coconut milk

½ chicken bouillon cube

3 curry leaves (optional)

1 pound white fish fillet, such as cod, haddock or whiting

8 ounces raw or cooked shrimp

1 small head lettuce, shredded

½ cup bean sprouts

3 scallions, shredded

½ cucumber, sliced and shredded

shrimp crackers, to serve

1 Grind the cashews using a mortar and pestle or in a food processor with the shallots, lemon grass and garlic. Cook the noodles according to the instructions on the package.

3 Add the shrimp paste or fish sauce and curry paste, followed by the coconut milk, bouillon cube and curry leaves. Mix thoroughly and simmer for 10 minutes.

2 Heat the oil in a large wok or saucepan, add the contents of the mortar or food processor, and fry for 1–2 minutes or until the nuts begin to brown.

4 Cut the white fish into bite-size pieces. Place the fish and shrimp tails in a large frying basket, immerse in the simmering coconut stock, and cook for 3–4 minutes. Transfer the fish and shrimp tails to a serving platter with the salad and noodles and transfer the broth to a tureen or lidded pot and serve (see Cook's Tip).

COOK'S TIP

To serve, line a large serving platter with the shredded lettuce leaves. Arrange the bean sprouts, scallions and cucumber in neat piles, together with the cooked fish, shrimp and noodles. Serve the salad with a bowl of shrimp crackers and the broth in a lidded stoneware pot.

APPETIZERS

Olive and Anchovy Bites

These melt-in-the-mouth morsels store very well; freeze them for up to 3 months or they can be kept in an airtight container for up to 2 weeks before serving.

Makes 40–45

1 cup flour

8 tablespoons (1 stick) chilled butter

4 ounces finely grated cheese, such as
    Manchego, aged Cheddar or Gruyère

1 can (2 ounces) anchovy fillets in oil,
    drained and roughly chopped

½ cup pitted black olives,
    roughly chopped

½ teaspoon cayenne pepper

sea salt

1 Place the flour, butter, cheese, anchovies, olives and cayenne in a food processor and pulse until the mixture forms a firm dough.

2 Wrap the dough loosely in plastic wrap. Set aside in the refrigerator to chill for 20 minutes.

3 Unwrap the dough and turn it out onto a lightly floured surface. Knead lightly and roll it out thinly.

4 Cut the dough into 2 inch wide strips, then cut across each strip diagonally, in alternate directions, to make triangles. Transfer to baking sheets and bake at 400°F for 8–10 minutes, until golden. Cool on a wire rack. Sprinkle generously with sea salt before serving.

COOK'S TIP

For a change, sprinkle the olive and anchovy bites with finely grated Parmesan cheese or dust lightly with cayenne pepper before baking.

Smoked Salmon Crêpes with Pesto

These simple crêpes take no more than 10–15 minutes to prepare and are perfect for a special occasion. Smoked salmon is delicious with fresh basil and combines well with toasted pine nuts and a spoonful of crème fraîche.

INGREDIENTS

Makes 12–16

½ cup milk

1 cup self-rising flour

1 egg

2 tablespoons pesto sauce

vegetable oil, for frying

scant 1 cup crème fraîche

4 ounces smoked salmon

¼ cup pine nuts, toasted

salt and freshly ground black pepper

12–16 fresh basil sprigs, to garnish

3 Heat the vegetable oil in a large frying pan. Spoon the crêpe mixture into the heated oil in small heaps. Allow about 30 seconds for the crêpes to rise, then turn and cook briefly on the other side. Keep warm. Continue cooking the crêpes in batches until all the batter has been used up.

4 Arrange the crêpes on a serving plate and top each one with a spoonful of crème fraîche.

5 Cut the salmon into ½-inch strips and place on top of each crêpe. Scatter each crêpe with pine nuts and garnish with a sprig of fresh basil.

1 Pour half of the milk into a mixing bowl. Add the flour, egg, pesto sauce and seasoning and mix to a smooth batter.

2 Add the remainder of the milk and stir until evenly blended.

Seafood Crêpes

The combination of fresh and smoked haddock imparts a wonderful flavor to the filling.

Serves 4–6

For the crêpes

1 cup flour

pinch of salt

1 egg, plus 1 egg yolk

1¼ cups milk

1 tablespoon melted butter, plus extra for cooking

2–3 ounces Gruyère cheese, grated

curly salad greens, to serve

For the filling

8 ounces smoked haddock fillet

8 ounces fresh haddock fillet

1¼ cups milk

⅔ cup light cream or half-and-half

2 tablespoons butter

¼ cup flour

freshly grated nutmeg

2 hard-cooked eggs, shelled and chopped

salt and freshly ground black pepper

1 To make the crêpes, sift the flour and salt into a bowl. Make a well in the center and add the egg and egg yolk. Whisk the eggs, starting to incorporate some of the flour from around the edges.

2 Gradually add the milk, whisking all the time, until the batter is smooth and has the consistency of thin cream. Stir in the melted butter.

3 Heat a small crêpe pan or omelet pan until hot, then rub around the inside of the pan with a pad of paper towels dipped in melted butter.

4 Pour about 2 tablespoons of the batter into the pan, then tip the pan to coat the base evenly. Cook for about 30 seconds, until the underside of the crêpe is golden brown.

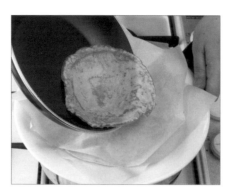

5 Flip the crêpe over and cook the other side until lightly browned. Repeat to make 12 crêpes, rubbing the pan with melted butter between cooking each crêpe. Stack the crêpes as you make them between sheets of waxed paper. Keep warm on a plate set over a pan of simmering water.

6 Put the smoked and fresh haddock fillets in a large pan. Add the milk and poach for 6–8 minutes, until just tender. Lift out the fish using a slotted spoon and, when cool enough to handle, remove the skin and any bones. Reserve the milk.

7 Pour the light cream or half-and-half into a measuring cup, then strain enough of the reserved milk into the cup to make the total quantity of 2 cups.

8 Melt the butter in a pan, stir in the flour and cook gently for 1 minute. Gradually mix in the milk mixture, stirring continuously, to make a smooth sauce. Cook for 2–3 minutes, until thickened. Season with salt, pepper and nutmeg. Roughly flake the haddock and fold into the sauce with the eggs. Let cool.

9 Divide the filling among the crêpes. Fold the sides of each crêpe into the center, then roll them up so that the filling is completely enclosed.

10 Butter four or six individual ovenproof dishes and arrange 2–3 filled crêpes in each, or butter one large dish for all the crêpes. Brush with melted butter and cook in a preheated oven at 350°F for 15 minutes. Sprinkle on the Gruyère and cook for another 5 minutes, until the crêpes are warmed through. Serve hot with a few curly salad greens.

VARIATION

For variety, add cooked, peeled shrimp, smoked mussels or cooked fresh, shelled mussels to the filling, instead of the chopped hard-cooked eggs.

Sautéed Scallops

Scallops go well with all sorts of sauces, but simple cooking is the best way to enjoy their flavor.

INGREDIENTS

Serves 4

1 pound shelled scallops

2 tablespoons butter

2 tablespoons dry white vermouth

1 tablespoon finely chopped fresh parsley

salt and freshly ground black pepper

1 Rinse the scallops under cold running water to remove any sand or grit and pat dry using paper towels. Season them lightly with salt and pepper.

2 In a frying pan large enough to hold the scallops in one layer, heat half the butter until it begins to color. Sauté the scallops for 3–5 minutes, turning, until golden brown on both sides and just firm to the touch. Remove to a serving platter and cover to keep warm.

3 Add the vermouth to the hot frying pan, swirl in the remaining butter, add the parsley and pour the sauce over the scallops. Serve immediately.

Garlicky Scallops and Shrimp

Scallops and shrimp are found all along the Atlantic and Mediterranean coasts of France and are enjoyed in every region. This method of cooking is a typical Provençal recipe.

INGREDIENTS

Serves 2–4

6 large shelled scallops

6–8 large raw shrimp, peeled

flour, for dusting

2–3 tablespoons olive oil

1 garlic clove, finely chopped

1 tablespoon chopped fresh basil

2–3 tablespoons lemon juice

salt and freshly ground black pepper

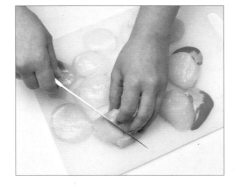

1 Rinse the scallops under cold running water to remove any sand or grit. Pat them dry using paper towels and cut in half horizontally. Season the scallops and shrimp with salt and pepper and dust lightly with flour, shaking off the excess.

2 Heat the oil in a large frying pan over a high heat and add the scallops and shrimp.

3 Reduce the heat to medium-high and cook for 2 minutes, then turn the scallops and shrimp. Add the garlic and basil, shaking the pan to distribute them evenly. Cook for another 2 minutes until the scallops are golden and just firm to the touch. Sprinkle on the lemon juice and toss to blend.

VARIATION

To make a richer sauce, transfer the cooked scallops and shrimp to a warmed plate. Pour ¼ cup dry white wine into the frying pan and boil to reduce by half. Add 1 tablespoon unsalted butter, whisking until it melts and the sauce thickens slightly. Pour the sauce over the scallops and shrimp and serve.

Scallops Wrapped in Prosciutto

This is a delicious summer recipe for cooking on the barbecue.

INGREDIENTS

Serves 4

24 medium-size scallops, without corals, prepared for cooking

lemon juice

8–12 slices prosciutto

olive oil

freshly ground black pepper

lemon wedges, to serve

1 Preheat the broiler or prepare a charcoal fire. Sprinkle the scallops with lemon juice. Cut the prosciutto into long strips. Wrap one strip around each scallop. Thread them onto 8 skewers.

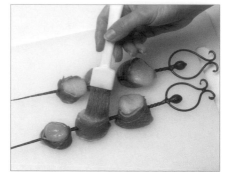

2 Brush with oil. Arrange on a baking sheet if broiling. Cook about 4 inches from the heat under a preheated broiler for 3–5 minutes on each side or until the scallops are opaque and tender. Alternatively, cook over charcoal, turning once, until the scallops are opaque and tender.

3 Set 2 skewers on each plate. Sprinkle the scallops with freshly ground black pepper and serve with lemon wedges.

COOK'S TIP

The edible parts of the scallop are the round white muscle and the coral or roe. When preparing fresh scallops, keep the skirt—the frilly part—for making stock.

Mussels Steamed in White Wine

This is the best and easiest way to serve the small, tender mussels, bouchots, which are farmed along much of the French coastline. Serve with plenty of crusty French bread to dip in the juices.

INGREDIENTS

Serves 4

4–4½ pounds mussels

1¼ cups dry white wine

4–6 large shallots, finely chopped

bouquet garni

freshly ground black pepper

1 Discard any broken mussels and those with open shells that do not close immediately when tapped sharply. Under cold running water, scrape the mussel shells with a knife to remove any barnacles and pull out the stringy "beards." Soak the mussels in several changes of cold water for at least 1 hour.

2 In a large heavy flameproof casserole, combine the white wine, shallots, bouquet garni and plenty of pepper. Bring to a boil over medium-high heat and cook for 2 minutes.

3 Add the mussels to the casserole, cover tightly and cook, shaking and tossing the pan occasionally, for 5 minutes or until the mussels have opened. Discard any mussels that have not opened.

4 Using a slotted spoon, divide the mussels among 4 warmed soup plates. Tilt the casserole a little and hold for a few seconds to let any sand sink to the bottom and settle. Alternatively, strain the cooking liquid through clean muslin into a bowl.

5 Spoon or pour the cooking liquid over the mussels and serve immediately.

VARIATION

For Mussels with Cream Sauce, cook the shellfish as described here, but transfer the mussels to a warmed bowl and cover to keep warm. Strain the cooking liquid through a muslin-lined sieve into a large saucepan and boil for about 7–10 minutes to reduce by half. Stir in 6 tablespoons whipping cream and 2 tablespoons chopped fresh parsley, then add the mussels. Cook for about 1 more minute to reheat the mussels.

Grilled Sardines

Fresh sardines have plenty of flavor, so they are at their best when cooked in a simple way.

INGREDIENTS

Serves 4

8 sardines, about 2 ounces each

sea salt

2 lemons, halved, to serve

1 Gut the sardines, but leave on the heads and tails. With a sharp knife, slash each side of all the sardines diagonally three times.

2 Place the sardines on a broiler pan and sprinkle with sea salt. Cook under a broiler preheated to high for 4 minutes on each side, until the flesh is cooked and the skin is blistered and just beginning to char.

3 Transfer to a serving dish and serve immediately with the lemon halves to squeeze over.

Salt-cured Salmon

This delicious treatment is a good alternative to smoked salmon.

INGREDIENTS

Serves 10

½ cup sea salt

3 tablespoons superfine sugar

1 teaspoon chili powder

1 teaspoon freshly ground black pepper

3 tablespoons chopped fresh cilantro

2 salmon fillets, about 9 ounces each

flat leaf parsley, to garnish

garlic mayonnaise, to serve

1 In a bowl, combine the salt, sugar, chili powder, pepper and cilantro. Rub the mixture into the flesh of each salmon fillet.

2 Place one of the fillets, skin side down, in a shallow glass dish. Place the other fillet on top, with the skin side up. Cover with foil, then place a weight on top.

3 Chill for 48 hours, turning the fish every 8 hours or so and basting it with the liquid that forms in the dish.

COOK'S TIP

Make the most of the leftover salmon skin by turning it into delicious crunchy strips: After slicing the salt-cured salmon, scrape any remaining fish off the skin and discard. Cut the skin into ½-inch-wide strips. Fry for 1 minute in hot oil until crisp and browned. Drain on paper towels and let cool. Serve as a garnish for the salt-cured salmon or as a tapas dish in its own right.

4 Drain the salmon well and transfer to a board. Using a sharp knife, slice it diagonally into wafer-thin slices. Arrange on plates and garnish with sprigs of parsley. Serve with garlic mayonnaise.

Deep-fried Whitebait

A spicy coating on these fish gives this favorite dish a crunchy bite.

Serves 6

1 cup flour

½ teaspoon curry powder

½ teaspoon ground ginger

½ teaspoon ground cayenne pepper

pinch of salt

2½ pounds fresh or frozen
   whitebait, thawed

vegetable oil, for deep-frying

lemon wedges, to garnish

1 Combine the flour, spices and salt in a large bowl.

2 Coat the fish in the seasoned flour and shake off any excess.

3 Heat the oil in a large heavy saucepan until it reaches a temperature of 375°F. Fry the whitebait in batches for 2–3 minutes until the fish is golden and crispy.

4 Drain well on absorbent paper towels. Serve hot, garnished with lemon wedges.

Sesame Shrimp Toasts

Serve about four triangles each with a soy sauce dip.

INGREDIENTS

Serves 6

6 ounces cooked shrimp, peeled
   and deveined

2 scallions, finely chopped

1-inch piece fresh ginger, grated

2 garlic cloves, crushed

½ cup cornstarch

2 teaspoons soy sauce, plus extra
   for dipping

6 slices stale bread from a small loaf,
   crusts removed

½ cup sesame seeds

vegetable oil, for deep-frying

1 Place the shrimp, scallions, ginger and garlic cloves into a food processor fitted with a metal blade. Add the cornstarch and soy sauce and work the ingredients into a thick paste.

2 Spread the bread slices evenly with the paste and sprinkle with the sesame seeds, making sure that they stick to the paste. Cut the slices into triangles and chill for 30 minutes.

3 Heat the oil for deep-frying in a large heavy pan until it reaches a temperature of 375°F. Using a slotted spoon, lower half the toasts into the oil, sesame seed side down, and fry for 2–3 minutes, turning over for the last minute. Drain on absorbent paper towels. Keep the toasts warm while frying the remainder.

4 Serve the toasts with the soy sauce for dipping.

COOK'S TIP
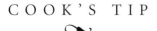

If you do not have a deep-fat thermometer, check that the oil is at the right temperature by tossing a stale bread cube into it. If it turns golden in 30 seconds, the temperature is just right.

Monkfish Parcels

These little dumplings of spiced fish taste delicious with the dressing of tomato oil.

INGREDIENTS

Serves 4

1½ cups flour

2 eggs

skinless monkfish fillet, 4 ounces, diced

grated rind of 1 lemon

1 garlic clove, chopped

1 small fresh red chili, seeded and sliced

3 tablespoons chopped fresh parsley

2 tablespoons light cream or half-and-half

flour, for dusting

salt and freshly ground black pepper

For the tomato oil

2 tomatoes, skinned, seeded and
   finely diced

3 tablespoons extra virgin olive oil

2 tablespoons fresh lemon juice

1 Place the flour, eggs and ½ teaspoon salt in a food processor; pulse until the mixture forms a soft dough. Knead gently for 2–3 minutes, until smooth, then wrap in plastic wrap. Chill for 20 minutes.

2 Place the monkfish, lemon rind, garlic, chili and parsley in the clean food processor and process until very finely chopped. Add the cream, with plenty of salt and pepper, and process again to form a very thick purée.

3 Make the tomato oil by stirring the diced tomato with the olive oil and lemon juice in a bowl. Add salt to taste. Cover and chill.

4 Roll out the dough on a lightly floured surface and cut out 32 rounds, using a 1½-inch cookie cutter. Divide the filling among half the rounds, then cover with the remaining rounds. Pinch the edges tightly to seal, excluding as much air as possible.

5 Bring a large saucepan of water to the simmering point and poach the parcels, in batches, for 2–3 minutes, or until they rise to the surface. Drain and serve hot, drizzled with the tomato oil.

Crab and Ricotta Tartlets

Use the meat from a freshly cooked crab, weighing about 1 pound, if you can. Otherwise, look for frozen brown and white crab meat.

INGREDIENTS

Serves 4

2 cups flour

8 tablespoons (1 stick) butter, diced

about ¼ cup ice water

1½ cups ricotta

1 tablespoon grated onion

2 tablespoons grated Parmesan cheese

½ teaspoon mustard powder

2 eggs, plus 1 egg yolk

8 ounces crab meat

2 tablespoons chopped fresh parsley

½–1 teaspoon anchovy paste

1–2 teaspoons lemon juice

salt and cayenne pepper

salad greens, to garnish

1 Sift the flour and a good pinch of salt into a mixing bowl, add the diced butter and rub it in with your fingertips, until the mixture resembles fine bread crumbs. Gradually stir in enough ice water to make a firm dough.

2 Turn the dough onto a floured surface and knead lightly. Roll out the pastry and use to line four 4-inch tartlet tins. Prick the bases with a fork, then chill in the refrigerator for 30 minutes.

3 Line the pastry shells with waxed paper and fill with baking beans. Bake in a preheated oven at 400°F for 10 minutes, then remove the paper and beans. Return to the oven and bake for another 10 minutes.

4 Place the ricotta, grated onion, Parmesan and mustard in a bowl and beat until soft. Gradually beat in the eggs and egg yolk.

5 Gently stir in the crab meat and chopped parsley, then add the anchovy paste, lemon juice, and salt and cayenne pepper, to taste.

6 Remove the tarts from the oven and reduce the temperature to 350°F. Spoon the filling into the shells and bake for 20 minutes, until set and golden brown. Serve hot with a garnish of salad greens.

Crab Savory

This scrumptious, baked seafood dish is rich and creamy.

INGREDIENTS

Serves 4

2 tablespoons butter

1 small onion, finely chopped

½ cup fresh brown bread crumbs

8 ounces crab meat

⅔ cup sour cream

2–3 teaspoons prepared mustard

pinch of cayenne pepper

squeeze of lemon juice

½ cup finely grated Cheddar cheese

salt

1 Melt the butter in a saucepan over medium heat, then cook the onion gently for 2–3 minutes, until it is soft but not brown.

2 Stir the bread crumbs, crab meat, sour cream and prepared mustard into the onions. Add a generous sprinkling of cayenne pepper, lemon juice and salt to taste. Heat through gently, stirring carefully.

3 Spoon the crab mixture into a baking dish, sprinkle the grated cheese over the top and place under a preheated, hot broiler until golden and bubbling.

Smoked Mackerel Pâté

The pâté can be flavored with horse-radish, if desired.

INGREDIENTS

Serves 4

10 ounces smoked mackerel fillet, skinned

6 tablespoons sour cream

8 tablespoons (1 stick) unsalted butter, softened

2 tablespoons chopped fresh parsley

1–2 tablespoons lemon juice

freshly ground black pepper

endive leaves and parsley, to garnish

fingers of toast, to serve

1 Remove any fine bones from the mackerel fillet, then mash it with a fork.

2 Work the sour cream and butter into the mackerel until smooth. Stir in the parsley and add lemon juice and pepper to taste.

3 Pack the mackerel mixture into a dish or bowl, then cover tightly and chill for 6–8 hours or overnight.

4 About 30 minutes before serving, remove the pâté from the refrigerator to let it return to room temperature. To serve, spoon onto individual plates and garnish with endive leaves and parsley. Serve with fingers of toast.

COOK'S TIP

For a less rich (and lower-calorie) version of this pâté, substitute 7 ounces low-fat cream cheese or sieved cottage cheese for the sour cream.

Sole Goujons with Lime Mayonnaise

*This simple dish can be rustled up
very quickly. It also makes an
excellent light lunch or supper.*

Serves 4

scant 1 cup mayonnaise

1 small garlic clove, crushed

2 teaspoons capers, rinsed and chopped

2 teaspoons chopped gherkins

grated rind and juice of 1 lime

1 tablespoon finely chopped
    fresh cilantro

1½ pounds sole fillets, skinned

2 eggs, beaten

2 cups fresh white bread crumbs

oil, for deep-frying

salt and freshly ground black pepper

lime wedges, to serve

1 To make the lime mayonnaise,
combine the mayonnaise,
garlic, capers, gherkins, lime rind
and juice and chopped cilantro.
Season with salt and pepper to
taste. Transfer to a serving bowl
and chill until required.

2 Cut the sole fillets into finger-
length strips. Dip each strip
first into the beaten egg, then into
the bread crumbs.

3 Heat the oil in a deep-fat fryer
to 350°F. Add the fish strips, in
batches, and fry until they are
golden brown and crisp. Drain
well on paper towels and keep
warm while you cook the
remaining strips.

4 Pile the goujons onto warmed
serving plates and serve with
the lime wedges for squeezing lime
juice onto them. Hand the sauce
around separately.

Spicy Fish Rösti

*You can also serve these fish cakes
crisp and hot for lunch or supper
with a mixed green salad.*

Serves 4

12 ounces large, firm waxy potatoes

12 ounces salmon or cod fillet, skinned
    and boned

3–4 scallions, finely chopped

1 teaspoon grated fresh ginger

2 tablespoons chopped fresh cilantro

2 teaspoons lemon juice

2–3 tablespoons sunflower oil

salt and cayenne pepper

cilantro sprigs, to garnish

lemon wedges, to serve

1 Cook the potatoes with their
skins on in a pan of boiling
salted water for 10 minutes. Drain
and let cool for a few minutes.

2 Meanwhile, finely chop the
salmon and put it into a bowl.
Stir in the chopped scallions,
grated ginger, chopped cilantro
and lemon juice. Season to taste
with salt and cayenne pepper.

3 When the potatoes are cool
enough to handle, peel off the
skins and grate the potatoes
coarsely. Gently stir the grated
potato into the fish mixture.

4 Form the fish mixture into
12 cakes, pressing the mixture
together and leaving the edges
slightly rough.

5 Heat the oil in a large frying
pan and fry the fish cakes, a
few at a time, for 3 minutes on
each side, until golden brown and
crisp. Drain on paper towels. Serve
hot, garnished with sprigs of
cilantro and with lemon wedges
for squeezing the juice on top.

Ceviche

This makes an excellent appetizer. With the addition of sliced avocado, it could make a light summer lunch.

INGREDIENTS

Serves 6

1 pound mackerel fillets, cut into ½-inch
   pieces
1½ cups freshly squeezed lime or lemon
   juice
8 ounces tomatoes, chopped
1 small onion, very finely chopped
2 drained canned jalapeño chilies or
   4 serrano chilies, rinsed and chopped
¼ cup olive oil
½ teaspoon dried oregano
2 tablespoons chopped fresh cilantro
salt and freshly ground black pepper
lemon wedges and fresh cilantro sprigs,
   to garnish
stuffed green olives sprinkled with
   chopped cilantro, to serve

1 Put the fish into a glass dish and pour in the lime or lemon juice, making sure that the fish is completely covered. Cover and chill for 6 hours, turning once, by which time the fish will be opaque, "cooked" by the juice.

COOK'S TIP

For a more delicately flavored ceviche, you can use a white fish, such as sole.

2 When the fish is opaque, lift it out of the juice and set it aside.

3 Combine the tomatoes, onion, chilies, olive oil, oregano and cilantro in a bowl. Add salt and pepper to taste, then pour in the reserved juice from the mackerel. Mix well and pour over the fish.

4 Cover the dish and return the ceviche to the refrigerator for about 1 hour to let the flavors blend. Ceviche should not be served too cold. Let it stand at room temperature for 15 minutes before serving. Garnish with lemon wedges and cilantro sprigs, and serve with stuffed olives sprinkled with chopped cilantro.

Glazed Garlic Shrimp

This is a fairly simple and quick dish to prepare. It is best to peel the shrimp, as this helps them to absorb maximum flavor. Serve with a salad as an appetizer or as a main course with a selection of vegetables and other accompaniments.

INGREDIENTS

Serves 4

1 tablespoon vegetable oil

3 garlic cloves, roughly chopped

3 tomatoes, chopped

½ teaspoon salt

1 teaspoon crushed dried red chilies

1 teaspoon lemon juice

1 tablespoon mango chutney

1 fresh green chili, chopped

15–20 cooked jumbo shrimp, peeled and deveined

fresh cilantro sprigs, 4 unpeeled, cooked jumbo shrimp and 2 scallions, chopped, to garnish

1 In a medium saucepan, heat the oil and add the chopped garlic cloves.

2 Lower the heat and add the chopped tomatoes along with the salt, crushed chilies, lemon juice, mango chutney and chopped fresh chili.

3 Finally, add the shrimp, turn up the heat and stir-fry them quickly, until heated through.

4 Transfer to a warmed serving dish. Serve garnished with fresh cilantro sprigs, unpeeled jumbo shrimp and chopped scallions, if desired.

COOK'S TIP

This is a very fiery dish—if you would prefer it less hot, carefully seed the chili before chopping and reduce the crushed chilies to a pinch.

Smoked Salmon Terrine with Lemons

Lemons can be cut and sliced in so many ways. This melt-in-the-mouth smoked salmon terrine gives a time-honored side dish an intriguing new twist.

INGREDIENTS

Serves 6

4 sheets of leaf gelatin

¼ cup water

14 ounces smoked salmon, sliced

1½ cups cream cheese

½ cup crème fraîche

2 tablespoons dill mustard

juice of 1 lime

For the garnish

2 lemons

piece of cheesecloth

raffia, for tying

2 Set aside enough of the remaining smoked salmon to make a middle layer the length of the pan. Chop the rest finely by hand or in a food processor. Beat together the cream cheese, crème fraîche and dill mustard with the chopped smoked salmon until everything is well combined.

4 Tap the pan to expel any trapped air. Fold over the over-hanging salmon slices to cover the top. Cover with plastic wrap and chill for at least 4 hours.

5 Make the garnish. Cut 1 lemon in half horizontally. Wrap each half in a small square of muslin. Gather the muslin at the rounded end of the lemon and tie neatly with raffia.

1 Soak the gelatin in the water in a small bowl until softened. Meanwhile, line a 1-pound loaf pan with plastic wrap. Use some of the smoked salmon to line the pan, laying the slices horizontally across the base and up the sides and leaving enough overlap to fold over the top of the filling.

3 Squeeze out the gelatin and melt gently in a small saucepan with the lime juice. Add to the smoked salmon mixture and mix thoroughly. Spoon half the mixture into the lined pan. Lay the reserved smoked salmon slices on the mixture along the length of the pan, then spoon on the rest of the filling and smooth the top.

6 Cut a small "V" from the side of the other lemon. Repeat at ¼ inch intervals. Turn out the terrine, then slice. Garnish with muslin-wrapped lemons and lemon "leaves."

Char-grilled Squid

Enjoy these tender bites of succulent squid right off the barbecue.

Serves 4

2¼ pounds prepared squid

6 tablespoons olive oil

juice of 1–2 lemons

3 garlic cloves, crushed

¼ teaspoon chili flakes

¼ cup chopped fresh parsley

lemon slices, to garnish

1 Reserve the squid tentacles, then, using a small, sharp knife, score the flesh into a diagonal pattern.

2 Place all the squid in a shallow, non-metallic dish. To make the marinade, thoroughly combine the olive oil, lemon juice, crushed garlic and chili flakes in a bowl.

3 Pour the marinade over the squid and put in the refrigerator for a minimum of 2 hours, stirring occasionally.

4 Lift the squid from the dish and reserve the marinade. Cook the squid on a barbecue for 2 minutes on each side, turning them frequently and brushing with the marinade until the outside is golden brown and crisp, with soft, moist flesh inside. Put the squid in a serving dish.

5 Bring the remaining marinade to a boil in a small pan, stir in the chopped parsley, then pour it over the squid. Garnish with lemon slices and serve immediately.

Monkfish Brochettes

These brochettes are colourful as well as full of flavour.

Serves 4

1½ pounds monkfish, skinned and boned

12 strips bacon

2 small zucchini

1 yellow or orange bell pepper, seeded and
  cut into 1-inch cubes

saffron rice, to serve

For the marinade

6 tablespoons olive oil

grated rind of ½ lime

3 tablespoons lime juice

2 tablespoons dry white wine

¼ cup chopped fresh mixed herbs, such as
  dill, chives and parsley

1 teaspoon honey

freshly ground black pepper

1 To make the marinade, combine the olive oil, lime rind and juice, wine, chopped herbs, honey and pepper in a bowl, then set aside.

2 Cut the monkfish into 1-inch cubes. Stretch the strips of bacon with the back of a knife, then cut each one in half and wrap around the monkfish cubes.

COOK'S TIP

If you are using wooden skewers, soak them in cold water before threading the fish and vegetables, so that they do not char when the brochettes are cooking.

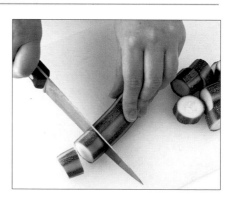

3 Pare strips of peel from the zucchini to create a striped effect, then cut into 1-inch chunks.

4 Thread the fish rolls onto skewers alternately with the zucchini and pepper. Place in a dish. Pour in the marinade and set aside in a cool place for 1 hour. Lift out the skewers, then broil for about 10 minutes, turning and basting occasionally with the marinade. Serve with saffron rice.

Thai Fish Cakes

Bursting with the flavor of chilies and lime, these little fish cakes make a wonderful appetizer.

Serves 4

1 pound firm white fish fillets, such as cod or haddock
3 scallions, sliced
2 tablespoons chopped fresh cilantro
2 tablespoons Thai red curry paste
1 fresh green chili, seeded and chopped
2 teaspoons grated lime rind
1 tablespoon lime juice
2 tablespoons peanut oil
salt
crisp lettuce leaves, shredded scallions, fresh red chili slices, cilantro sprigs and lime wedges, to serve

1 Cut the fish into 1-inch chunks, then place in a blender or food processor.

2 Add the scallions, cilantro, red curry paste, green chili, lime rind and juice to the fish. Season with salt to taste. Process until finely ground.

3 Using lightly floured hands, divide the fish mixture into 16 pieces and shape each one into a small cake about 1½ inches across. Place the fish cakes on a plate, cover with plastic wrap and chill for about 2 hours until firm. Heat a wok over high heat until hot. Add the oil and swirl it around quickly to heat it.

4 Fry the fish cakes, a few at a time, for 6–8 minutes, turning them carefully, until they are evenly browned. Drain each batch on paper towels and keep hot while you are cooking the remainder. Serve on a bed of crisp lettuce leaves with shredded scallions, red chili slices, cilantro sprigs and lime wedges.

Seafood Wontons with Cilantro Dressing

These tasty wontons resemble tortellini. Water chestnuts add a light crunch to the filling.

Serves 4

8 ounces cooked shrimp, peeled
   and deveined
4 ounces white crab meat
4 canned water chestnuts, finely diced
1 scallion, finely chopped
1 small green chili, seeded and
   finely chopped
¼ teaspoon grated fresh ginger
1 egg, separated
20–24 wonton wrappers
salt and freshly ground black pepper
cilantro leaves, to garnish

For the cilantro dressing
2 tablespoons rice vinegar
1 tablespoon chopped, pickled ginger
6 tablespoons olive oil
1 tablespoon soy sauce
3 tablespoons chopped cilantro
2 tablespoons finely diced red bell pepper

1 Finely dice the shrimp and place them in a bowl. Add the crab meat, water chestnuts, scallion, chili, ginger and egg white. Season with salt and pepper to taste and stir well.

2 Place a wonton wrapper on a board. Put about 1 teaspoon of the filling just above the center of the wrapper. With a pastry brush, moisten the edges of the wrapper with a little beaten egg yolk. Bring the bottom of the wrapper up over the filling. Press gently to expel any air, then seal the wrapper neatly in a triangle.

3 For a more elaborate shape, bring the two side points up over the filling, overlap the points and pinch the ends firmly together. Space the filled wontons an inch apart on a large baking sheet lined with waxed paper, so that they do not stick together.

4 Half fill a large saucepan with water. Bring to simmering point. Add the filled wontons, a few at a time, and simmer for 2–3 minutes or until the wontons float to the surface. When ready, the wrappers will be translucent and the filling should be cooked. Remove the wontons with a large slotted spoon, drain them briefly, then spread them on trays. Keep warm while you cook the remaining wontons.

5 Make the cilantro dressing by whisking all the ingredients together in a bowl. Divide the wontons among serving dishes, drizzle with the dressing and serve, garnished with a handful of cilantro leaves.

Grilled Green Mussels with Cumin

Green-shelled mussels have a more distinctive flavor than the small, black variety. Keep the empty shells to use as individual salt and pepper holders for fishy meals.

INGREDIENTS

Serves 4

3 tablespoons fresh parsley

3 tablespoons fresh cilantro

1 garlic clove, crushed

pinch of ground cumin

2 tablespoons unsalted butter, softened

¼ cup brown bread crumbs

12 green mussels or 24 small mussels, on the half shell

freshly ground black pepper

chopped fresh parsley, to garnish

1 Finely chop the fresh parsley and cilantro.

2 Beat the garlic, herbs, cumin and butter together with a wooden spoon.

3 Stir in the bread crumbs and freshly ground black pepper.

4 Spoon a little of the mixture onto each mussel and grill for 2 minutes. Serve garnished with chopped fresh parsley.

Welsh Rarebit with Anchovies

This classic snack or appetizer has been adapted and updated to include salty anchovies.

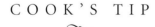
INGREDIENTS

Serves 4

1 can (2 ounces) canned anchovies,
   drained

12 tablespoons (1½ sticks) butter

6 slices of bread, crusts removed

4 large egg yolks

1¼ cups heavy cream

pinch of cayenne pepper

salt and freshly ground black pepper

1 tablespoon chopped fresh parsley,
   to garnish

1 In a food processor fitted with a metal blade, process the anchovy fillets with two-thirds of the butter. Toast the bread, spread with the anchovy butter, set aside and keep warm.

COOK'S TIP
~
If you find canned anchovies too salty, soak them briefly in cold water before processing them with the butter.

2 Melt the remaining butter in a small heavy saucepan and beat in the egg yolks.

3 Take off the heat and add the cream. Season to taste, then replace on a low heat. Stir until the sauce is thick. Pour onto the toast and sprinkle with the cayenne pepper. Garnish with the chopped fresh parsley.

SALADS

Spinach Salad with Bacon and Shrimp

Serve this hot salad with plenty of crusty bread for mopping up the delicious juices.

Serves 4

7 tablespoons olive oil

2 tablespoons sherry vinegar

2 garlic cloves, finely chopped

1 teaspoon Dijon mustard

12 cooked jumbo shrimp

4 strips bacon

about 4 ounces fresh young
    spinach leaves

½ head oak leaf lettuce, roughly torn

salt and freshly ground black pepper

1 To make the dressing, whisk together 6 tablespoons of the olive oil with the vinegar, garlic, mustard and seasoning in a small pan. Heat gently until thickened slightly, then keep warm.

2 Carefully peel the shrimp, leaving the tails intact. Set aside.

3 Heat the remaining oil in a frying pan and fry the bacon until golden and crisp, stirring occasionally. Add the shrimp and stir-fry for a few minutes, until warmed through.

4 While the bacon and shrimp are cooking, arrange the spinach and torn oak leaf lettuce leaves on four individual serving plates.

5 Spoon the bacon and shrimp onto the leaves, then pour on the hot dressing. Serve immediately.

COOK'S TIP

Sherry vinegar lends its pungent flavor to this delicious salad. You can buy it at most large supermarkets and delicatessens.

Shrimp and Artichoke Salad

Artichokes are very popular in Louisiana, where this recipe comes from—and the local cooks are quite willing to use canned hearts.

INGREDIENTS

Serves 4

1 garlic clove

2 teaspoons Dijon mustard

¼ cup red wine vinegar

⅔ cup olive oil

3 tablespoons shredded fresh basil leaves
    or 2 tablespoons finely chopped
    fresh parsley

1 red onion, very finely sliced

12 ounces cooked peeled shrimp

1 can (14 ounces) artichoke hearts

½ head iceberg lettuce

salt and freshly ground black pepper

1 Coarsely chop the garlic, then crush it to a pulp with 1 teaspoon salt, using the flat of a heavy knife blade.

2 Mix the garlic and mustard to a paste, then beat in the vinegar and finally the olive oil, beating hard to make a thick, creamy dressing. Season with freshly ground black pepper and, if necessary, additional salt.

3 Stir the fresh basil into the dressing, followed by the finely sliced red onion. Let stand for 30 minutes at room temperature, then stir in the shrimp and chill in the refrigerator for 1 hour or until ready to serve.

4 Drain the artichoke hearts and halve each one. Shred the lettuce finely.

5 Make a bed of lettuce on a serving platter or 4 individual salad plates and spread the artichoke hearts over it.

6 Immediately before serving, pour the shrimp and sliced onion and their marinade on top of the salad.

Grilled Salmon and Spring Vegetable Salad

Spring is the time to enjoy sweet young vegetables. Cook them briefly, cool to room temperature, dress and serve with a piece of lightly grilled salmon topped with sorrel and quails' eggs.

INGREDIENTS

Serves 4

12 ounces small new potatoes, scrubbed
    or scraped

4 quails' eggs

4 small carrots, peeled

1 can (4 ounces) baby corn

1 cup sugar snap peas, trimmed

1 cup fine green beans, trimmed

2 small zucchini

2 small patty pan squash (optional)

½ cup French dressing

4 salmon fillets, each weighing 5 ounces,
    skinned

4 ounces sorrel or young spinach,
    stems removed

salt and freshly ground black pepper

2 Cover the quails' eggs with boiling water and cook for 8 minutes. Refresh under cold water, shell and cut in half.

3 Bring a saucepan of salted water to a boil, add all the other vegetables, except the sorrel, and cook for about 3 minutes. Drain well. Place the hot vegetables and potatoes in a salad bowl, moisten with a little French dressing and let cool.

5 Place the sorrel in a stainless steel or enamel saucepan with ¼ cup French dressing, cover and soften over low heat for 2 minutes. Strain and cool the sorrel to room temperature. Moisten the vegetables set aside in step 3 with the remaining dressing.

6 Divide the potatoes and vegetables between 4 large plates, then position a piece of salmon on one side of each plate. Finally, place a spoonful of sorrel on each piece of salmon and top with 2 halves of a quail's egg. Season to taste and serve at room temperature.

1 Bring the potatoes to a boil in salted water and cook for 15–20 minutes. Drain, cover and keep warm.

4 Brush the salmon fillets with French dressing and broil for 6 minutes, turning once.

COOK'S TIP

For French dressing, combine 6 tablespoons olive oil, 2 table-spoons white wine vinegar, 1 teaspoon Dijon mustard, 1 teaspoon sugar, 1 crushed garlic clove and seasoning to taste.

Warm Salmon Salad

Light and fresh, this salad is perfect for an al fresco summer lunch. Serve it immediately, or you'll find the salad greens will lose their bright color and texture.

INGREDIENTS

Serves 4

1 pound salmon fillet, skinned
2 tablespoons sesame oil
grated rind of ½ orange
juice of 1 orange
1 teaspoon Dijon mustard
1 tablespoon chopped fresh tarragon
3 tablespoons peanut oil
1 cup fine green beans, trimmed
2 ounces mixed salad greens, such as
   young spinach leaves, radicchio, frisée
   and oak leaf lettuce
1 tablespoon toasted sesame seeds
salt and freshly ground black pepper

1 Cut the salmon into bite-size pieces, then make the dressing. Combine the sesame oil, orange rind and juice, mustard, chopped tarragon and seasoning in a bowl. Set aside.

2 Heat the peanut oil in a frying pan. Add the salmon pieces and fry for 3–4 minutes, until lightly browned but still tender inside.

3 Meanwhile, blanch the green beans in boiling salted water for about 5–6 minutes, until they are tender, but still crisp.

4 Add the dressing to the salmon, toss together gently and cook for 30 seconds. Remove the pan from the heat.

5 Arrange the salad greens on 4 serving plates. Drain the beans and toss over the leaves. Spoon over the salmon and cooking juices and serve immediately, sprinkled with the toasted sesame seeds.

Salmon and Tuna Parcels

You will need fairly large smoked salmon slices as they are wrapped around a light tuna mixture before being served on a vibrant salad.

INGREDIENTS

Serves 4

2 tablespoons low-fat plain yogurt

1 tablespoon sun-dried tomato paste

1 teaspoon whole-grain honey mustard

grated rind and juice of 1 lime

1 can (7 ounces) tuna in brine, drained

5 ounces smoked salmon slices

salt and freshly ground black pepper

fresh mint leaves, to garnish

For the salad

3 tomatoes, sliced

2 kiwi fruit, peeled and sliced

¼ cucumber, cut into julienne sticks

For the mint vinaigrette

1 tablespoon wine vinegar

3 tablespoons olive oil

1 tablespoon chopped fresh mint

COOK'S TIP
~

Although healthy eating guidelines recommend reducing the amount of fat, particularly saturated fat, in the diet, salad dressings made with polyunsaturated or monounsaturated oil, such as olive oil, can and should be included, in sensible moderation.

This recipe is not high in calories, but if weight control is a real issue, use an oil-free dressing instead of vinaigrette.

1 Mix the yogurt, tomato paste and mustard in a bowl. Stir in the grated lime rind and juice. Add the tuna, with black pepper to taste, and mix well.

2 Spread out the salmon slices on a board and spoon some of the tuna mixture onto each piece.

3 Roll up or fold the smoked salmon into neat parcels. Carefully press the edges together to seal.

4 Make the salad. Arrange the tomato and kiwi slices on 4 serving plates. Scatter on the cucumber sticks.

5 Make the vinaigrette. Put all the ingredients in a screw-top jar, season with salt and pepper and shake vigorously. Spoon a little vinaigrette over each salad.

6 Arrange 3–4 salmon parcels on each salad, garnish with the mint leaves and serve.

Avocado and Smoked Fish Salad

Avocado and smoked fish make an excellent combination and, flavored with herbs and spices, create a delectable salad.

INGREDIENTS

Serves 4

4 tablespoons (½ stick) butter
½ onion, finely sliced
1 teaspoon mustard seeds
8 ounces smoked mackerel, flaked
2 tablespoons chopped fresh cilantro
2 firm tomatoes, skinned and chopped
1 tablespoon lemon juice
salt and freshly ground black pepper

For the salad

2 avocado pears
½ cucumber
1 tablespoon lemon juice
2 firm tomatoes
1 green chili

1 Melt the butter in a frying pan, add the sliced onion and mustard seeds and fry for about 5 minutes, until the onion is soft, but not colored.

2 Add the fish, cilantro leaves, tomatoes and lemon juice and cook over low heat for 2–3 minutes. Remove from the heat and set aside to cool.

3 Make the salad. Peel and thinly slice the avocado pears and slice the cucumber. Put into a bowl and sprinkle with the lemon juice.

4 Slice the tomatoes. Seed and finely chop the chili.

5 Place the fish mixture in the center of a serving plate.

6 Arrange the avocado pears, cucumber and tomatoes around the fish. Alternatively, spoon a quarter of the fish mixture onto each of 4 serving plates and divide the avocados, cucumber and tomatoes equally. Sprinkle with the chopped chili and a little salt and pepper and serve.

Warm Fish Salad with Mango Dressing

This salad is best served during the summer months, preferably out-of-doors. The dressing combines the flavor of rich mango with hot chili, ginger and lime.

INGREDIENTS

Serves 4

1 loaf of French bread

4 black bream or porgy, each weighing about 10 ounces

1 tablespoon vegetable oil

1 mango

½-inch piece fresh ginger

1 fresh red chili, seeded and finely chopped

2 tablespoons lime juice

2 tablespoons chopped fresh cilantro

6 ounces young spinach

5 ounces bok choy

6 ounces cherry tomatoes, halved

1 Cut the French loaf into 8-inch lengths. Slice length-ways, then cut into thick fingers. Place the bread on a baking sheet and dry in a preheated oven at 350°F for 15 minutes. Slash the fish deeply on both sides with a sharp knife and moisten with oil. Cook under a preheated broiler or on a barbecue for 6 minutes, turning once.

2 Peel and pit the mango. Slice the flesh and place half of it in a food processor. Peel and finely grate the ginger, then add to the food processor with the chili, lime juice and cilantro. Process until smooth. Adjust to a pouring consistency with 2–3 tablespoons water.

3 Wash the salad greens and spin dry, then divide them equally between 4 serving plates. Place the fish on the leaves. Spoon on the mango dressing and finish with slices of mango and cherry tomato halves. Serve with the fingers of crispy French bread.

C O O K ' S   T I P

Other fish suitable for this salad include salmon, monkfish, tuna, sea bass and halibut. Use fillets, cutlets or steaks.

Mediterranean Salad with Basil

A type of Salade Niçoise with pasta, this conjures up all the sunny flavors of the Mediterranean.

Serves 4

8 ounces chunky pasta shapes

1 cup green beans

2 large ripe tomatoes

2 ounces fresh basil leaves

1 can (7 ounces) tuna fish in oil, drained and roughly flaked

2 hard-cooked eggs, shelled and sliced or quartered

1 can (2 ounces) anchovy fillets, drained

salt and freshly ground black pepper

capers and black olives, to garnish

For the dressing

6 tablespoons extra virgin olive oil

2 tablespoons white wine vinegar or lemon juice

2 garlic cloves, crushed

½ teaspoon Dijon mustard

2 tablespoons chopped fresh basil

1 Whisk all the ingredients for the dressing together, season with salt and pepper and let infuse while you make the salad.

2 Cook the pasta in plenty of boiling salted water according to the manufacturer's instructions. Drain well and set aside to cool.

3 Trim the green beans and blanch them in boiling salted water for 3 minutes. Drain, then refresh in cold water.

4 Slice or quarter the tomatoes and arrange on the base of a bowl. Moisten with a little dressing and cover with a quarter of the basil leaves. Then cover with the beans. Moisten with a little more dressing and cover with a third of the remaining basil.

5 Cover with the pasta tossed in a little more dressing, half the remaining basil and the roughly flaked tuna.

6 Arrange the sliced eggs on top. Finally, scatter over the anchovy fillets, capers and black olives. Pour on the remaining dressing and garnish with the remaining basil. Serve immediately. Do not be tempted to chill this salad—all the flavor will be dulled.

COOK'S TIP

Olives marinated in oil flavored with garlic, herbs and lemon peel would add an extra-special touch to this salad. Choose plump, black olives that are fully ripened. Marinated olives are available at large supermarkets and delicatessens, or you could prepare them yourself.

Thai Seafood Salad

This unusual seafood salad with chili, lemon grass and fish sauce is light and refreshing.

Serves 4

8 ounces ready-prepared squid

8 ounces raw tiger shrimp

8 scallops, shelled

8 ounces firm white fish

2–3 tablespoons olive oil

small mixed lettuce leaves and cilantro
sprigs, to serve

For the dressing

2 small fresh red chilies, seeded and
finely chopped

2-inch piece lemon grass, finely chopped

2 fresh kaffir lime leaves, shredded

2 tablespoons Thai fish sauce

2 shallots, thinly sliced

2 tablespoons lime juice

2 tablespoons rice vinegar

2 teaspoons superfine sugar

2 Heat a wok or large frying pan until hot. Add the oil and swirl it around, then add the shrimp and stir-fry for 2–3 minutes, until pink. Transfer to a large bowl. Stir-fry the squid and scallops for 1–2 minutes, until opaque. Remove and add to the shrimp. Stir-fry the white fish for 2–3 minutes. Remove and add to the cooked seafood. Reserve any juices.

3 Put all the dressing ingredients in a small bowl with the reserved juices from the wok or frying pan and mix well.

4 Pour the dressing over the seafood and toss gently. Arrange the greens and cilantro sprigs on 4 individual plates, then spoon the seafood on top. Serve immediately.

1 Prepare the seafood. Slit open the squid bodies, cut into square pieces, then score the flesh in a crisscross pattern with a sharp knife. Halve the tentacles, if necessary. Peel and devein the shrimp. Remove the dark beard-like fringe and tough muscle from the scallops. Cube the white fish.

Gado Gado

Gado Gado is a traditional Indonesian salad around which friends and family gather to eat. Fillings are chosen and wrapped in a lettuce leaf. The parcel is then dipped in a spicy peanut sauce and eaten, usually with the left hand. Salad ingredients vary according to what is in season.

INGREDIENTS

Serves 4

2 medium potatoes, peeled

3 eggs

1½ cups green beans, trimmed

1 head romaine lettuce

4 tomatoes, cut into wedges

1 cup bean sprouts

½ cucumber, peeled and cut into fingers

5 ounces giant white radish, peeled and grated

6 ounces tofu, cut into large dice

12 ounces large cooked peeled shrimp

1 small bunch fresh cilantro

salt

For the spicy peanut sauce

½ cup smooth peanut butter

juice of ½ lemon

2 shallots or 1 small onion, finely chopped

1 garlic clove, crushed

1–2 small fresh red chilies, seeded and finely chopped

2 tablespoons fish sauce (optional)

⅔ cup coconut milk, canned or fresh

1 tablespoon superfine sugar

1 To make the peanut sauce, combine the ingredients in a food processor until smooth.

2 Bring the potatoes to a boil in salted water and simmer for 20 minutes. Bring a second pan of salted water to a boil. To avoid using too many pans, cook the eggs and beans in the same pan.

3 Lower the eggs into the boiling water in the second pan; then, after 6 minutes, add the beans in a steamer for another 6 minutes. (Hard-cooked eggs should cook for a total of 12 minutes.) Cool the potatoes, eggs and green beans under cold running water.

4 Wash and spin the lettuce leaves and use the outer leaves to line a large platter. Pile the remainder on one side of the platter.

5 Slice the potatoes. Shell and quarter the eggs. Arrange the potatoes, eggs, beans and tomatoes in separate piles. Arrange the other salad ingredients and the shrimp in a similar way to cover the platter. Garnish with the cilantro.

6 Transfer the spicy peanut sauce to an attractive bowl and bring to the table with the salad.

HANDLING CHILIES

Red chilies are considered to be sweeter and hotter than green ones. Smaller varieties of both red and green are likely to be more pungent than larger varieties. You can lessen the intensity of a fresh chili by splitting it open and removing the white seed-bearing membrane. The residue released when chilies are cut can cause serious irritation to the skin. Be sure to wash your hands thoroughly after handling raw chilies and avoid touching your eyes or any sensitive skin areas.

Seafood Salad with Fragrant Herbs

This tasty medley of seafood and noodles is a meal in itself.

INGREDIENTS

Serves 4–6

1 cup fish stock or water

12 ounces squid, cleaned and cut into rings

12 raw jumbo shrimp, peeled and deveined

12 scallops, cleaned

2 ounces bean thread noodles, soaked in
    warm water for 30 minutes

½ cucumber, cut into thin sticks

1 stalk lemon grass, finely chopped

2 kaffir lime leaves, finely shredded

2 shallots, finely sliced

juice of 1–2 limes

2 tablespoons fish sauce

2 tablespoons chopped scallion

2 tablespoons cilantro leaves

12–15 mint leaves, roughly torn

4 red chilies, seeded and sliced

cilantro sprigs, to garnish

1 Pour the fish stock into a medium-size saucepan, set over high heat and bring to a boil.

2 Place each type of seafood individually in the stock and cook for a few minutes. Remove and set aside.

3 Drain the bean thread noodles and cut them into short lengths, about 2 inches long. Combine the noodles with the cooked seafood.

4 Add the cucumber, lemon grass, kaffir lime leaves, shallots, lime juice, fish sauce, scallion, cilantro, mint leaves and chilies and combine well. Serve garnished with the cilantro sprigs.

Pomelo Salad

Pomelo is a large, pear-shaped fruit that resembles a grapefruit.

INGREDIENTS

Serves 4-6

2 tablespoons vegetable oil

4 shallots, finely sliced

2 garlic cloves, finely sliced

1 large pomelo

1 tablespoon roasted peanuts

4 ounces cooked peeled shrimp

4 ounces cooked crab meat

10–12 small mint leaves

2 scallions, finely sliced

2 red chilies, seeded and finely sliced

cilantro leaves, to garnish

shredded fresh coconut (optional)

For the dressing

2 tablespoons fish sauce

1 tablespoon brown sugar

2 tablespoons lime juice

1 Make the dressing. Whisk together the fish sauce, brown sugar and lime juice and set aside.

2 Heat the oil in a small frying pan, add the shallots and garlic and fry for 3–4 minutes, until they are golden. Remove from the pan and set aside.

3 Peel the pomelo and break the flesh into small pieces, taking care to remove any membranes.

4 Coarsely grind the peanuts, then combine with the pomelo flesh, shrimp, crab meat, mint leaves and the fried shallot mixture. Toss the salad in the dressing and serve sprinkled with the scallions, red chilies, cilantro leaves and shredded coconut, if using.

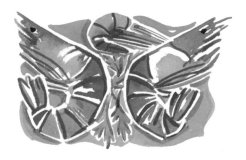

Russian Salad

Russian salad became fashionable in the hotel dining rooms of the 1920s and 1930s. Originally it consisted of lightly cooked vegetables, eggs, shellfish and mayonnaise. Today we find it diced in plastic containers at supermarket delis. This version recalls better days and plays on the theme of the Fabergé egg.

INGREDIENTS

Serves 4

16 large button mushrooms

12 ounces cooked peeled shrimp

½ cup mayonnaise

1 tablespoon lemon juice

1 large gherkin, chopped, or
   2 tablespoons capers

1 cup fava beans, shelled

8–10 small new potatoes, scrubbed
   or scraped

4 carrots, trimmed and peeled

1 cup baby corn

1 cup baby turnips, trimmed

1 tablespoon olive oil, preferably French
   or Italian

4 eggs, hard-cooked and shelled

6–8 canned anchovy fillets, cut into fine
   strips

salt and freshly ground black pepper

paprika, to garnish

1 Slice the mushrooms, then cut into matchsticks. Mix with the shrimp. Combine the mayonnaise and lemon juice and fold half into the mushrooms and shrimp, add the gherkin or capers and season.

2 Bring a large saucepan of salted water to a boil, add the fava beans and cook for 3 minutes. Drain and cool under cold running water, then pinch the beans between thumb and forefinger to release them from their tough skins. Boil the potatoes for 20 minutes and the remaining vegetables for 6 minutes. Drain and cool under running water.

3 Moisten the vegetables with olive oil and divide between 4 shallow bowls. Spoon on the dressed shrimp and place a hard-cooked egg in the center. Decorate the egg with strips of anchovy and sprinkle with paprika. Serve the remaining mayonnaise separately.

Melon and Crab Salad

A perfect summer salad when crab and melon are in generous supply.

INGREDIENTS

INGREDIENTS

Serves 6

1 pound fresh cooked crab meat

½ cup mayonnaise

3 tablespoons sour cream or
   plain yogurt

2 tablespoons olive oil

2 tablespoons fresh lemon or lime juice

2–3 scallions, finely chopped

2 tablespoons finely chopped
   fresh cilantro

¼ teaspoon cayenne pepper

1½ cantaloupe or small honeydew melons

3 medium endives

salt and freshly ground black pepper

fresh cilantro sprigs, to garnish

1 Pick over the crab meat very carefully, removing any bits of shell or cartilage. Leave the pieces of crab meat as large as possible.

2 In a medium-size bowl, combine mayonnaise, sour cream or yogurt, olive oil, lemon or lime juice, scallions, chopped cilantro and cayenne pepper and season to taste with salt and pepper. Mix well, then fold the crab meat into this dressing.

3 Halve the melons and remove and discard the seeds. Cut the melons into thin slices, then remove the rind.

4 Divide the salad between 6 individual serving plates, making a decorative design with the melon slices and whole endive leaves. Place a mound of dressed crab meat on each plate and garnish the salads with one or two fresh cilantro sprigs.

Millionaire's Lobster Salad

When money is no object and you're in a decadent mood, this salad will satisfy your every whim. It is ideally served with a cool Chardonnay, Chablis or Pouilly-Fuissé wine.

Serves 4

1 medium lobster, live or cooked

1 bay leaf

1 sprig thyme

1½ pounds new potatoes, scrubbed

2 ripe tomatoes

4 oranges

½ head chicory or radicchio

1 head Boston lettuce

¼ cup extra virgin olive oil

1 can (7 ounces) young artichokes in
  brine, quartered

salt

1 small bunch tarragon, chervil or flat
  leaf parsley, to garnish

For the dressing

2 tablespoons frozen concentrated orange
  juice, thawed

6 tablespoons (¾ stick) unsalted butter,
  diced

cayenne pepper

1 If the lobster needs to be cooked, add to a large pan of salted water with the bay leaf and thyme. Bring to a boil and simmer for 15 minutes. Cool under running water. Twist off the legs and claws, and separate the tail piece from the body section. Break the claws open with a hammer and remove the meat intact. Cut the tail piece open from the underside with a pair of kitchen shears. Slice the meat and set aside.

2 Bring the potatoes to a boil in salted water and simmer for 20 minutes. Drain, cover and keep warm. Cover the tomatoes with boiling water and set aside for 20 seconds to loosen their skins. Cool under running water and slip off the skins. Halve the tomatoes, discard the seeds, then cut the flesh into large dice.

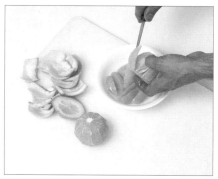

3 To segment the oranges, remove the peel from the top, bottom and sides with a serrated knife. With a small paring knife, loosen the orange segments by cutting between the flesh and the membranes, holding the fruit over a small bowl.

4 To make the dressing, measure the thawed orange juice into a glass bowl and set it over a saucepan containing 1 inch of simmering water. Heat the juice for 1 minute, remove from the heat, then whisk in the butter, a little at a time, until the dressing reaches a coating consistency. Season to taste with salt and a pinch of cayenne pepper, cover and keep warm.

5 Wash the salad greens and spin dry. Dress with olive oil, then divide between 4 large serving plates. Moisten the potatoes, artichokes and orange segments with olive oil and distribute them among the salad greens. Lay the sliced lobster over the salad, spoon on the warm butter dressing, add the diced tomato and decorate with sprigs of fresh tarragon. Serve at room temperature.

Smoked Trout Salad

Horseradish is as good a partner to smoked trout as it is to roast beef. In this recipe it combines with yogurt to make a deliciously piquant light salad dressing.

INGREDIENTS

Serves 4

1 head oak leaf or red leaf lettuce

6–8 small tomatoes, cut into thin
    wedges

½ cucumber, peeled and thinly sliced

4 smoked trout fillets, about 7 ounces
    each, skinned and flaked

For the dressing

pinch of English mustard powder

3–4 teaspoons white wine vinegar

2 tablespoons light olive oil

scant ½ cup plain yogurt

about 2 tablespoons grated fresh or
    bottled horseradish

pinch of superfine sugar

1 First, make the dressing. Combine the mustard powder and vinegar, then gradually whisk in the oil, yogurt, horseradish and sugar. Set aside for 30 minutes.

COOK'S TIP

Salt should not be necessary in this recipe because of the saltiness of the smoked trout.

2 Place the lettuce leaves in a large bowl. Stir the dressing again, then pour half of it over the leaves and toss them lightly using two spoons.

3 Arrange the lettuce on 4 individual plates with the tomatoes, cucumber and trout. Spoon on the remaining dressing and serve immediately.

Tuna and Bean Salad

This substantial salad makes a good light meal and can be assembled quickly from canned ingredients.

INGREDIENTS

Serves 4–6

1 can (14 ounces) cannellini or borlotti
   beans
2 cans (7 ounces each) tuna, drained
¼ cup extra virgin olive oil
2 tablespoons fresh lemon juice
1 tablespoon chopped fresh parsley
3 scallions, thinly sliced
salt and freshly ground black pepper

1 Pour the beans into a large strainer and rinse under cold water. Drain well. Place in a serving dish.

2 Break the tuna into fairly large flakes and arrange over the beans in the serving dish.

3 In a small bowl make the dressing by combining the oil with the lemon juice. Season with salt and pepper and stir in the parsley. Mix well. Pour onto the beans and tuna.

4 Sprinkle with the sliced scallion. Toss the salad well before serving.

Niçoise Salad

There are probably as many versions of this salad as there are cooks in Provence. With chunks of good French bread, this regional classic makes a wonderful summer lunch or light supper.

INGREDIENTS

Serves 4–6

2 cups green beans

1 pound new potatoes, peeled and cut into
    1-inch pieces

white wine vinegar and olive oil,
    for sprinkling

1 small head romaine lettuce, washed,
    dried and torn into bite-sized pieces

4 ripe plum tomatoes, quartered

1 small cucumber, peeled, seeded
    and diced

1 green or red bell pepper, thinly sliced

4 hard-cooked eggs, shelled and quartered

24 Niçoise or black olives

1 can (8 ounces) tuna in brine, drained

1 can (2 ounces) anchovy fillets in olive
    oil, drained

basil leaves, to garnish

garlic croûtons, to serve

For the anchovy vinaigrette

4 teaspoons Dijon mustard

1 can (2 ounces) anchovy fillets in
    olive oil, drained

1 garlic clove, crushed

¼ cup lemon juice or white wine vinegar

½ cup sunflower oil

½ cup extra virgin olive oil

freshly ground black pepper

1 First, make the anchovy vinaigrette. Place the mustard, anchovy fillets and garlic in a bowl and blend together by pressing the garlic and anchovies against the sides of the bowl. Season well with pepper. Using a small whisk, blend in the lemon juice or vinegar. Slowly whisk in the sunflower oil in a thin stream and then the olive oil, whisking until the dressing is smooth and creamy.

2 Alternatively, put all the dressing ingredients except the oils in a food processor fitted with a metal blade and process. With the machine running, slowly add the oils, in a thin stream, until the vinaigrette is thick and creamy.

3 Drop the green beans into a large saucepan of boiling water and boil for 3 minutes until tender, yet crisp. Transfer the beans to a colander with a slotted spoon, then rinse under cold running water. Drain again and set aside.

4 Add the potatoes to the same boiling water, reduce the heat and simmer for 10–15 minutes, until just tender, then drain. Sprinkle with a little vinegar and olive oil and a spoonful of the anchovy vinaigrette.

5 Arrange the lettuce on a platter, top with the tomatoes, cucumber and pepper, then add the green beans and potatoes.

6 Arrange the eggs, olives, tuna and anchovies on top and garnish with the basil leaves. Drizzle the remaining anchovy vinaigrette on top of the salad and serve with garlic croûtons.

COOK'S TIP

To make garlic croûtons, slice a loaf of French bread or a larger loaf of bread into 1-inch cubes. Place the bread in a single layer on a baking sheet and bake in a preheated 350°F oven for 7–10 minutes or until golden brown, turning once. Rub the toast with a raw garlic clove and serve hot or let cool, then store in an airtight container to serve at room temperature.

Shrimp Salad with Curry Dressing

Curry spices add an unexpected twist to this salad. Warm flavors combine especially well with sweet shrimp and grated apple.

INGREDIENTS

Serves 4

1 ripe tomato
½ head iceberg lettuce, shredded
1 small onion
1 small bunch fresh cilantro
1 tablespoon lemon juice
1 pound cooked peeled shrimp
1 apple, peeled
salt
8 whole cooked shrimp, 8 lemon wedges
    and 4 sprigs fresh cilantro, to garnish

For the dressing
5 tablespoons mayonnaise
1 teaspoon mild curry paste
1 tablespoon ketchup
2 tablespoons water

1 To peel the tomato, pierce the skin with a knife and immerse in boiling water for 20 seconds. Drain and cool under running water. Peel off the skin. Halve the tomato, push the seeds out with your thumb and discard them. Cut the flesh into large dice.

2 Finely shred the lettuce, onion and cilantro. Add the tomato, moisten with lemon juice and season with salt.

3 To make the dressing, combine the mayonnaise, curry paste and ketchup in a small bowl. Add the water to thin the dressing and season to taste with salt.

4 Combine the shrimp with the dressing. Quarter and core the apple and grate into the mixture.

5 Distribute the shredded lettuce and onion mixture between 4 plates or bowls. Pile the shrimp mixture in the center of each and garnish with 2 whole shrimp, 2 lemon wedges and a sprig of cilantro.

COOK'S TIP

Fresh cilantro is inclined to wilt if it is not kept in water. Store it in the refrigerator, in a jar of water covered with a plastic bag, and it will stay fresh for several days.

Eggplant Salad with Dried Shrimp

An appetizing and unusual salad that you will find yourself making over and over again.

INGREDIENTS

Serves 4–6

2 eggplant

1 tablespoon oil

2 tablespoons dried shrimp, soaked
   and drained

1 tablespoon coarsely chopped garlic

2 tablespoons freshly squeezed lime juice

1 teaspoon brown sugar

2 tablespoons fish sauce

1 hard-cooked egg, shelled and chopped

4 shallots, finely sliced into rings

cilantro leaves and 2 red chilies, seeded
   and sliced, to garnish

1 Grill or roast the eggplant until charred and tender.

2 When the eggplant is cool enough to handle, peel off the skin and slice the flesh.

3 Heat the oil in a small frying pan, add the drained shrimp and garlic and fry for 3–4 minutes, until golden. Remove from the pan and set aside.

4 To make the dressing, put the lime juice, brown sugar and fish sauce in a small bowl and whisk together.

5 To serve, arrange the eggplant on a serving dish. Top with the egg, shallots and dried shrimp mixture. Drizzle on the dressing and garnish with the cilantro leaves and red chilies.

COOK'S TIP

For an interesting variation, try using salted ducks' or quails' eggs, cut in half, instead of chopped hens' eggs.

Thai Dipping Sauce

This is a delicious and traditional accompaniment to Hot Coconut Shrimp and Pawpaw Salad.

INGREDIENTS

Makes ½ cup

1 tablespoon vegetable oil

½-inch square shrimp paste, or
   1 tablespoon fish sauce

2 garlic cloves, finely sliced

¾-inch piece fresh ginger, peeled and
   finely chopped

3 small red chilies, seeded and chopped

1 tablespoon finely chopped cilantro root
   or stem

4 teaspoons sugar

3 tablespoons dark soy sauce

juice of ½ lime

1 Heat the vegetable oil in a wok, add the shrimp paste, garlic, ginger and chilies and soften without coloring, for 1–2 minutes.

2 Remove from the heat and add the cilantro, sugar, soy sauce and lime juice. The sauce will keep in a screw-top jar for up to 10 days.

Hot Coconut Shrimp and Pawpaw Salad

This exotic salad may be served with many Asian beef and chicken dishes.

INGREDIENTS

Serves 4-6

8 ounces raw or cooked shrimp, peeled
   and deveined

2 ripe pawpaws

8 ounces mixed salad greens and young
   spinach

1 firm tomato, skinned, seeded and
   roughly chopped

3 scallions, shredded

1 small bunch cilantro, shredded,
   1 large chili, sliced, and 1 turnip, carved,
   to garnish

Thai Dipping Sauce, to serve

For the dressing

1 tablespoon creamed coconut

2 tablespoons boiling water

6 tablespoons vegetable oil

juice of 1 lime

½ teaspoon hot chili sauce

2 teaspoons fish sauce (optional)

1 teaspoon sugar

1 To make the dressing, place the creamed coconut in a screw-top jar and add the boiling water to soften. Add the vegetable oil, lime juice, chili sauce, fish sauce, if using, and sugar. Shake well and set aside. Do not refrigerate.

2 If using raw shrimp, cover with cold water in a saucepan, bring to a boil and simmer for no longer than 2 minutes. Drain and set aside.

3 To prepare the pawpaws, cut each in half from top to bottom and remove the black seeds with a teaspoon. Peel off the outer skin and cut the flesh into even-size pieces. Wash the salad greens and toss in a bowl. Add the other ingredients. Pour on the dressing, garnish with the cilantro, chili and turnip, and serve with Thai Dipping Sauce.

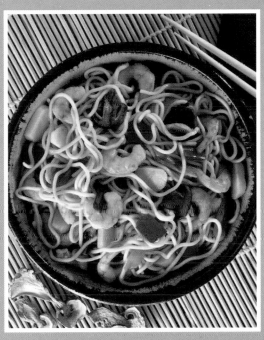

PASTA AND
RICE

Pasta with Tuna, Capers and Anchovies

This piquant sauce could be made without the addition of tomatoes— just heat the oil, add the other ingredients and heat through gently before tossing with the pasta.

Serves 4

2 cans tuna (7 ounces each) in oil

2 tablespoons olive oil

2 garlic cloves, crushed

1¾ pounds canned chopped tomatoes

6 canned anchovy fillets, drained

2 tablespoons capers in vinegar, drained

2 tablespoons chopped fresh basil

4 cups rigatoni or penne

salt and freshly ground black pepper

fresh basil sprigs, to garnish

1 Drain the oil from the tuna into a heavy saucepan, add the olive oil and heat gently until it stops "spitting."

2 Add the garlic and fry until golden. Stir in the tomatoes, lower the heat and simmer for 25 minutes, until thickened.

3 Flake the tuna and cut the anchovies in half. Stir into the sauce with the capers and chopped basil. Season well.

4 Cook the pasta in plenty of boiling salted water according to the manufacturer's instructions. Drain well and toss with the sauce. Garnish with fresh basil sprigs.

Farfalle with Smoked Salmon and Dill

This quick, luxurious and quite delicious sauce for pasta has now become very fashionable in Italy.

Serves 4

6 scallions, sliced

4 tablespoons (½ stick) butter

6 tablespoons dry white wine or vermouth

2 cups heavy cream

freshly grated nutmeg

8 ounces smoked salmon

2 tablespoons chopped fresh dill

freshly squeezed lemon juice

1 pound farfalle (pasta bows)

salt and freshly ground black pepper

fresh dill sprigs, to garnish

1 Slice the scallions finely. Melt the butter in a saucepan and fry the scallions for about 1 minute, until softened.

2 Add the wine and boil hard to reduce to about 2 tablespoons. Stir in the cream and add salt, pepper and nutmeg to taste. Bring to a boil and simmer for 2–3 minutes, until slightly thickened.

3 Cut the smoked salmon into 1-inch squares and stir into the sauce, together with the dill. Add a little lemon juice to taste. Keep warm.

4 Cook the pasta in plenty of boiling salted water as directed. Drain well. Toss with the sauce and serve immediately, garnished with sprigs of dill.

Tagliatelle with Smoked Salmon

This is a pretty pasta sauce that tastes as good as it looks. The light texture of the cucumber perfectly complements the fish. Different effects and color combinations can be achieved by using green, white or red tagliatelle—or even a mixture of all three.

INGREDIENTS

Serves 4

12 ounces dried or fresh tagliatelle

½ cucumber

6 tablespoons (¾ stick) butter

grated rind of 1 orange

2 tablespoons chopped fresh dill

1¼ cups light cream or half-and-half

1 tablespoon orange juice

4 ounces smoked salmon, skinned

salt and freshly ground black pepper

1 If using dried pasta, cook in lightly salted boiling water following the manufacturer's instructions on the package. If using fresh pasta, cook in lightly salted boiling water for 2–3 minutes or until just tender but still firm to the bite.

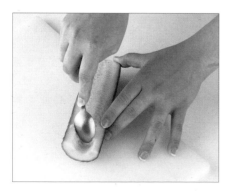

2 Using a sharp knife, cut the cucumber in half lengthwise. Using a small spoon, scoop out the cucumber seeds and discard.

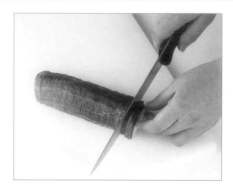

3 Turn the cucumber halves onto their flat sides and slice thinly.

4 Melt the butter in a heavy saucepan, add the grated orange rind and fresh dill and stir well. Add the cucumber and cook gently over low heat for about 2 minutes, stirring occasionally.

5 Add the cream, orange juice and seasoning to taste and simmer gently for 1 minute.

6 Meanwhile, cut the salmon into thin strips.

7 Stir the salmon into the sauce and heat through.

8 Drain the pasta thoroughly and toss it in the sauce. Serve immediately.

COOK'S TIP

A more economical way to make this special-occasion sauce is to use smoked salmon pieces, sold relatively inexpensively at most delicatessens and some supermarkets. (These are just scraps and awkwardly shaped pieces that are unsuitable for recipes requiring whole slices of smoked salmon.) Smoked trout is a less expensive alternative, but it lacks the rich flavor and color of smoked salmon.

Shrimp and Pasta Salad with Green Dressing

Anchovies need a nice strong dressing to match their flavor.

INGREDIENTS

Serves 4-6

4 anchovy fillets, drained

¼ cup milk

8 ounces squid

1 tablespoon chopped capers

1 tablespoon chopped gherkins

1–2 garlic cloves, crushed

⅔ cup plain yogurt

2–3 tablespoons mayonnaise

squeeze of lemon juice

1 small bunch watercress, chopped finely

2 tablespoons chopped fresh parsley

2 tablespoons chopped fresh basil

12 ounces fusilli (pasta spirals)

12 ounces cooked peeled shrimp

salt and freshly ground black pepper

1 Put the anchovies into a small bowl and cover with the milk. Let soak for 10 minutes. Pull the heads off the squid and remove and discard the quills. Peel the outer speckled skin from the bodies and rinse well. Cut into ¼-inch rings. Cut the tentacles from the heads, rinse under cold water and cut into ¼-inch slices.

2 To make the dressing, mix the capers, gherkins, garlic, yogurt, mayonnaise, lemon juice and fresh herbs in a bowl. Drain and chop the anchovies. Add to the dressing with the seasoning.

3 Drop the squid rings and tentacles into a large pan of boiling salted water. Lower the heat and simmer for 1–2 minutes (do not overcook or the squid will become tough). Remove with a slotted spoon. Cook the pasta in the same water according to the instructions on the package. Drain thoroughly.

4 Mix the shrimp and squid into the dressing in a large bowl. Add the pasta, toss and serve immediately. Alternatively, let cool and serve as a salad.

Noodles with Tomatoes and Shrimps

Influences from Italy and the East combine in this dish.

INGREDIENTS

Serves 4

12 ounces somen noodles

3 tablespoons olive oil

20 raw jumbo shrimp, peeled and
   deveined

2 garlic cloves, finely chopped

3–4 tablespoons sun-dried tomato paste

salt and freshly ground black pepper

For the garnish

handful of basil leaves

2 tablespoons sun-dried tomatoes in oil,
   drained and cut into strips

1 Cook the noodles in a large saucepan of boiling water until tender, following the directions on the package. Drain well.

2 Heat half the oil in a large frying pan. Add the shrimp and garlic and fry them over medium heat for 3–5 minutes, until the shrimp turn pink and are firm to the touch.

3 Stir in 1 tablespoon of the sun-dried tomato paste and mix well. Using a slotted spoon, transfer the shrimp to a bowl and keep hot.

4 Reheat the oil remaining in the pan. Stir in the rest of the oil with the remaining sun-dried tomato paste. You may need to add a spoonful of water if the mixture is very thick.

5 When the mixture starts to sizzle, toss in the well-drained noodles. Add salt and pepper to taste and mix well.

6 Return the shrimp to the pan and toss well to combine. Serve immediately, garnished with the basil leaves and strips of sun-dried tomatoes.

COOK'S TIP

Ready-made sun-dried tomato paste is widely available. However, you can make your own simply by processing bottled sun-dried tomatoes with their oil. You could also add a couple of anchovy fillets and some capers, if desired.

Linguine with Clams

Toss together this sauce for a real seafood flavor and serve with a light mixed salad. Canned clams make this a speedy sauce for those in a real hurry.

INGREDIENTS

Serves 4

12 ounces linguine (thin noodles)

2 tablespoons butter

2 leeks, thinly sliced

⅔ cup dry white wine

4 tomatoes, skinned, seeded and chopped

pinch of ground turmeric (optional)

1 can (9 ounces) clams, drained

2 tablespoons chopped fresh basil

¼ cup crème fraîche

salt and freshly ground black pepper

1 Cook the pasta following the instructions on the package.

2 Meanwhile, melt the butter in a small saucepan and fry the leeks for about 5 minutes until softened but not colored.

3 Add the wine, tomatoes and turmeric, if using, bring to a boil and boil until reduced by half.

4 Stir in the clams, basil, crème fraîche and seasoning to taste and heat through gently without allowing the sauce to boil.

5 Drain the pasta thoroughly and toss it in the sauce to coat. Serve immediately.

Macaroni with Jumbo Shrimp and Ham

This quick-and-easy recipe is an ideal lunch or supper dish.

INGREDIENTS

Serves 4

12 ounces macaroni

3 tablespoons olive oil

12 raw jumbo shrimp, peeled and deveined

1 garlic clove, chopped

6 ounces smoked ham, diced

⅔ cup red wine

½ small head radicchio, shredded

2 egg yolks, beaten

2 tablespoons chopped fresh flat leaf parsley

⅔ cup heavy cream

salt and freshly ground black pepper

shredded fresh basil, to garnish

1 Cook the pasta following the instructions on the package.

2 Meanwhile, heat the oil in a frying pan and cook the shrimp, garlic and ham for about 5 minutes, stirring occasionally, until the shrimp are tender.

3 Add the wine and radicchio, bring to a boil and boil rapidly until the juices are reduced by about half.

4 Stir in the egg yolks, parsley and cream and bring almost to a boil, stirring constantly, then simmer until the sauce thickens slightly. Season to taste.

5 Drain the pasta thoroughly and toss it in the sauce to coat. Serve immediately, garnished with shredded fresh basil.

COOK'S TIP

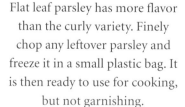

Flat leaf parsley has more flavor than the curly variety. Finely chop any leftover parsley and freeze it in a small plastic bag. It is then ready to use for cooking, but not garnishing.

Pasta with Scallops in Green Sauce

The striking colors of this dish make it irresistible.

INGREDIENTS

Serves 4

½ cup low-fat crème fraîche

2 teaspoons whole-grain mustard

2 garlic cloves, crushed

2–3 tablespoons fresh lime juice

¼ cup chopped fresh parsley

2 tablespoons snipped chives

12 ounces black tagliatelle

12 large prepared scallops

¼ cup white wine

⅔ cup fish stock

salt and freshly ground black pepper

lime wedges and parsley sprigs, to garnish

1 To make the green sauce, combine the crème fraîche, mustard, garlic, lime juice, herbs and seasoning in a bowl.

2 Cook the pasta in boiling salted water according to the package instructions. Drain well.

3 Slice the scallops in half, horizontally. Keep any coral whole. Put the wine and fish stock into a saucepan. Heat to simmering point. Add the scallops and cook very gently for 3–4 minutes.

4 Remove the scallops. Boil the wine and stock vigorously to reduce by half and add the green sauce to the pan. Heat gently to warm, replace the scallops and cook for 1 minute. Spoon the sauce over the pasta and garnish with lime wedges and parsley.

Pasta with Scallops in Tomato Sauce

Delicate and simple, this pasta dish makes a good appetizer or main dish.

Serves 4

1 pound long, thin pasta, such as fettucine or linguine

2 tablespoons olive oil

2 garlic cloves, finely chopped

1 pound prepared scallops, sliced in half horizontally

2 tablespoons chopped fresh basil

salt and freshly ground black pepper

fresh basil sprigs, to garnish

For the sauce

2 tablespoons olive oil

½ onion, finely chopped

1 garlic clove, finely chopped

2 cans (14 ounces each) peeled tomatoes

1 To make the sauce, heat the oil in a non-stick frying pan. Add the onion, garlic and a little salt, and cook for about 5 minutes, stirring occasionally, until just softened, but not colored.

2 Add the tomatoes with their juice, and crush with a fork. Bring to a boil, then lower the heat and simmer gently for 15 minutes. Remove the pan from the heat and set aside.

3 Bring a large pan of salted water to a boil. Add the pasta and cook until just tender to the bite, according to the instructions on the package.

4 Meanwhile, combine the oil and garlic in another non-stick frying pan and cook for about 30 seconds, until just sizzling. Add the scallops and ½ teaspoon salt and cook over high heat for about 3 minutes, tossing, until the scallops are cooked completely through.

5 Add the scallops to the tomato sauce. Season with salt and pepper to taste, then stir gently and keep warm.

6 Drain the pasta and rinse under hot water. Add the scallop sauce and the basil and toss thoroughly. Serve immediately, garnished with fresh basil sprigs.

Spaghettini with Vodka and Caviar

This is an elegant, yet easy, way to serve spaghettini. In Rome it is an after-theater favorite.

INGREDIENTS

Serves 4

¼ cup olive oil

3 scallions, thinly sliced

1 garlic clove, finely chopped

½ cup vodka

⅔ cup heavy cream

⅔ cup black or red caviar

1 pound spaghettini

salt and freshly ground black pepper

1 Heat the oil in a small frying pan. Add the scallions and garlic, and cook gently for 4–5 minutes, until softened.

2 Add the vodka and cream, and cook over low heat for about 5–8 more minutes.

3 Remove from the heat and stir in the caviar. Season with salt and pepper, as necessary.

4 Meanwhile, cook the pasta in a large pan of rapidly boiling salted water until tender, but still firm to the bite. Drain the pasta, and toss immediately to coat with the sauce. Serve immediately.

COOK'S TIP

The finest caviar is salted sturgeon roe. Red "caviar" is dog salmon roe, cheaper and often saltier than sturgeon roe.

Penne with Tuna and Mozzarella

This tasty sauce is quickly made from ingredients you are likely to have on hand, with the simple addition of fresh mozzarella and parsley. If possible, use tuna canned in olive oil.

INGREDIENTS

Serves 4

14 ounces penne, or other short pasta

1 tablespoon capers, in brine or salt

2 garlic cloves

3 tablespoons chopped fresh parsley

1 can (7 ounces) of tuna, drained

5 tablespoons olive oil

4 ounces mozzarella cheese, cut into small dice

salt and freshly ground black pepper

1 Bring a pan of salted water to the boil and cook the pasta according to package instructions.

2 Rinse the capers well in water. Chop them finely with the garlic. Combine with the parsley and the tuna. Stir in the oil, and season to taste.

3 Drain the pasta when it is just tender, but still firm to the bite. Transfer to a large frying pan. Add the tuna sauce and the diced mozzarella. Cook over medium heat, stirring constantly, until the cheese is just beginning to melt. Serve immediately.

Black Pasta with Squid Sauce

Tagliatelle flavored with squid ink looks amazing and tastes deliciously of the sea. You'll find it at good Italian delicatessens.

INGREDIENTS

Serves 4

½ cup olive oil

2 shallots, chopped

2 garlic cloves, crushed

3 tablespoons chopped fresh parsley

1½ pounds cleaned squid, cut into rings and rinsed

⅔ cup dry white wine

1 can (14 ounces) chopped tomatoes

½ teaspoon dried chili flakes or powder

1 pound black tagliatelle

salt and freshly ground black pepper

1 Heat the oil in a pan and add the shallots. Cook until pale golden in color, then add the garlic. When the garlic colors a little, add 2 tablespoons of the parsley, stir, then add the squid and stir again. Cook for 3–4 minutes, then add the wine.

2 Simmer for a few seconds, then add the tomatoes and chili flakes or powder and season with salt and pepper to taste. Cover and simmer gently for about 1 hour, until the squid is tender. Add more water if necessary.

3 Cook the pasta in plenty of boiling salted water, according to the instructions on the package, until tender, but still firm to the bite. Drain and return the pasta to the pan. Add the squid sauce and mix well. Sprinkle each serving with the remaining chopped parsley and serve immediately.

COOK'S TIP

The labeling of olive oil can be confusing. The oil is basically divided into two types—pure and virgin. The latter comes from the first pressing, but virgin olive oil is further sub-divided, according to its level of acidity. The least acidic and therefore the best oil is extra virgin. Use this quality for special dishes and salad dressings, but the next best oil—virgin— may be used for general cooking. Pure olive oil, although not in any way adulterated, lacks the unique flavor of virgin oil.

Tagliatelle with Saffron Mussels

Mussels in a saffron and cream sauce are served with tagliatelle in this recipe, but you can use any other pasta.

INGREDIENTS

Serves 4

4–4½ pounds mussels

⅔ cup dry white wine

2 shallots, chopped

12 ounces dried tagliatelle

2 tablespoons butter

2 garlic cloves, crushed

1 cup heavy cream

generous pinch of saffron strands, soaked
    in 2 tablespoons hot water

1 egg yolk

salt and freshly ground black pepper

2 tablespoons chopped fresh parsley,
    to garnish

1 Scrub the mussels under cold running water. Remove the beards. Discard any mussels with damaged shells or that do not shut immediately when sharply tapped.

2 Place the mussels in a large pan with the wine and shallots. Cover and cook over high heat, shaking the pan occasionally, for 5–8 minutes, until the mussels have opened. Drain the mussels, reserving the liquid. Discard any that remain closed. Shell all but a few of the mussels and keep warm.

3 Bring the reserved cooking liquid to a boil, then boil vigorously to reduce by about half. Strain through a fine sieve into a bowl to remove any grit.

4 Cook the tagliatelle in a pan of boiling salted water, according to the package instructions, until tender, but still firm to the bite.

5 Melt the butter in a pan and fry the garlic for 1 minute. Add the mussel liquid, cream and saffron. Heat gently, until the sauce thickens slightly. Remove from the heat and stir in the egg yolk, shelled mussels and seasoning.

6 Drain the pasta and transfer to serving bowls. Spoon on the sauce and sprinkle with chopped parsley. Garnish with the mussels in shells and serve immediately.

Sicilian Spaghetti with Sardines

A traditional dish from Sicily, with ingredients that are common to many parts of the Mediterranean.

INGREDIENTS

Serves 4

12 fresh sardines, cleaned and boned

1 cup olive oil

1 onion, chopped

¼ cup fresh dill, chopped

½ cup pine nuts

½ cup raisins, soaked in water

½ cup fresh bread crumbs

1 pound spaghetti

flour for dusting

salt

1 Wash the sardines and pat them dry with paper towels. Open them out flat, then cut in half lengthwise.

2 Heat 2 tablespoons of the oil in a pan, add the onion and fry until golden. Add the dill and cook gently for 1–2 minutes. Add the pine nuts and raisins and season with salt to taste. Dry-fry the bread crumbs in a frying pan until golden. Set aside.

3 Cook the spaghetti in boiling salted water according to the instructions on the package, until tender, but still firm to the bite. Heat the remaining oil in a pan. Dust the sardines with flour and fry in the hot oil for 2–3 minutes. Drain on paper towels.

4 Drain the spaghetti and return to the pan. Add the onion mixture and toss well to coat. Transfer the spaghetti mixture to a warmed serving platter and arrange the fried sardines on top. Sprinkle with the toasted bread crumbs and serve immediately.

COOK'S TIP

Sardines are actually baby pilchards and weigh about 4 ounces. They are covered in very fine scales that are most easily removed with your hand, rather than with a scaling knife. Hold the fish by the tail under cold running water and rub your thumb and fingers gently along the body down to the head.

Smoked Haddock and Pasta in Parsley Sauce

A creamy and delicious pasta dish with a crunchy almond topping.

INGREDIENTS

Serves 4

1 pound smoked haddock fillet

1 small leek or onion, sliced thickly

1¼ cups milk

1 bouquet garni (bay leaf, thyme and
parsley stalks)

2 tablespoons margarine

2 tablespoons flour

8 ounces pasta shells

2 tablespoons chopped fresh parsley

salt and freshly ground black pepper

½ cup toasted sliced almonds, to garnish

3 Put the margarine, flour and reserved milk into a pan. Bring to a boil and whisk constantly until smooth. Season, then add the fish and leek.

4 Cook the pasta in a large pan of boiling water until tender, but still firm to the bite. Drain and stir into the sauce with the chopped parsley. Serve immediately, scattered with almonds.

1 Remove all the skin and any bones from the haddock. Put into a pan with the leek, milk and bouquet garni. Bring to a boil, cover and simmer gently for 8–10 minutes, until the fish flakes easily.

2 Strain, reserving the milk for making the sauce, and discard the bouquet garni.

Baked Seafood Spaghetti

In this dish, each portion is baked and served in an individual parcel, which is then opened at the table. Use parchment paper or aluminum foil to make the parcels.

INGREDIENTS

Serves 4

1 pound fresh mussels

½ cup dry white wine

¼ cup olive oil

2 garlic cloves, finely chopped

1 pound tomatoes, fresh or canned, peeled and finely chopped

14 ounces spaghetti or other long pasta

8 ounces fresh, or frozen and thawed, uncooked peeled shrimp, deveined

2 tablespoons chopped fresh parsley

salt and freshly ground black pepper

1 Scrub the mussels well under cold running water, cutting off the beards with a small sharp knife. Discard any with broken shells or that do not close immediately when sharply tapped. Place the mussels and the wine in a large saucepan and heat until they open.

2 Lift out the mussels and remove to a side dish. Discard any that do not open. Strain the cooking liquid through clean muslin to remove any grit and reserve until needed.

3 In a medium saucepan, heat the oil and garlic together for 1–2 minutes. Add the tomatoes, and cook over medium to high heat until they soften. Stir in ¾ cup of the reserved cooking liquid from the mussels and simmer gently.

4 Meanwhile, cook the pasta in a large pan of boiling salted water, according to the package instructions, until tender, but still firm to the bite.

5 Just before draining the pasta, add the shrimp and parsley to the tomato sauce. Simmer for another 2 minutes or until the shrimp are cooked through. Taste and adjust the seasoning, if necessary. Remove from the heat and set aside. Drain the pasta.

6 Prepare 4 pieces of parchment paper approximately 12 x 18 inches in size. Place each sheet in the center of a shallow bowl. Transfer the drained pasta to a mixing bowl. Add the tomato sauce and mix well. Stir in the mussels.

7 Divide the pasta and seafood between the 4 pieces of paper, placing a mound in the center of each and twisting the paper ends together to make a closed packet. (The bowl under the paper will prevent the sauce from spilling while the paper parcels are being closed.) Arrange on a large baking sheet and bake at 300°F for 8–10 minutes. Place an unopened packet on each of 4 individual serving plates.

Fusilli with Smoked Trout

The smoked trout and creamy sauce blend beautifully with the still crunchy vegetables.

INGREDIENTS

Serves 4–6

2 carrots, cut into julienne sticks

1 leek, cut into julienne sticks

2 stalks celery, cut into julienne sticks

⅔ cup vegetable stock

8 ounces smoked trout fillets, skinned and
    cut into strips

8 ounces cream cheese

⅔ cup medium sweet white wine or fish
    stock

1 tablespoon chopped fresh dill or fennel

8 ounces long curly fusilli

salt and freshly ground black pepper

dill sprigs, to garnish

1 Put the carrots, leek and celery into a pan with the vegetable stock. Bring to a boil and cook quickly for 4–5 minutes, until the vegetables are tender and most of the stock has evaporated. Remove from the heat and add the smoked trout.

2 To make the sauce, put the cream cheese and wine or fish stock into a saucepan, heat and whisk until smooth. Season with salt and pepper. Add the chopped dill.

3 Cook the fusilli in a large pan of boiling salted water, according to the package instructions, until tender, but firm to the bite. Drain thoroughly.

4 Return the fusilli to the pan with the sauce, toss lightly and transfer to a serving bowl. Top with the cooked vegetables and trout. Serve immediately, garnished with dill sprigs.

Spaghetti with Hot-and-sour Fish

*A truly Chinese spicy taste is what
makes this sauce so different.*

INGREDIENTS

Serves 4

12 ounces spaghetti tricolore

1 pound monkfish, skinned

2 zucchini

1 fresh green chili, cored and seeded

1 tablespoon olive oil

1 large onion, chopped

1 teaspoon turmeric

1 cup peas, thawed if frozen

2 teaspoons lemon juice

5 tablespoons hoisin sauce

⅔ cup water

salt and freshly ground black pepper

dill sprig, to garnish

1 Cook the pasta in boiling
salted water according to the
instructions on the package, until
tender, but still firm to the bite.

2 Meanwhile, with a large sharp
knife, cut the monkfish into
bite-size pieces.

COOK'S TIP

This dish is quite low in calories,
so it is ideal for dieters. Hoisin
sauce is widely available at most
large supermarkets or Chinese
food stores.

3 Thinly slice the zucchini, then
finely chop the fresh, green
chili. Set aside.

4 Heat the oil in a large frying
pan and fry the onion for
5 minutes, until softened, but not
colored. Add the turmeric.

5 Add the chili, zucchini and
peas and fry over medium
heat for about 5 minutes, until the
vegetables have softened.

6 Stir in the fish, lemon juice,
hoisin sauce and water. Bring
to a boil, then simmer for about
5 minutes or until the fish is
tender. Season to taste.

7 Drain the pasta thoroughly and
transfer it to a serving bowl.
Toss in the sauce to coat. Serve
immediately, garnished with the
fresh sprig of dill.

Seafood Laska

For a special occasion serve creamy rice noodles in a spicy, coconut-flavored broth, topped with a selection of seafood. There is a fair amount of work involved in the preparation, but you can make the soup base ahead.

Serves 4

4 fresh red chilies, seeded and
  roughly chopped

1 onion, roughly chopped

1 piece balachan, the size of a stock cube

1 lemon grass stalk, chopped

1 small piece fresh ginger, roughly
  chopped

6 macadamia nuts or almonds

¼ cup vegetable oil

1 teaspoon paprika

1 teaspoon ground turmeric

2 cups stock or water

2½ cups coconut milk

fish sauce (see method)

12 raw jumbo shrimp, peeled and
  deveined

8 scallops

8 ounces prepared squid, cut into rings

12 ounces rice vermicelli or rice noodles,
  soaked in warm water until soft

salt and freshly ground black pepper

lime halves, to serve

For the garnish

¼ cucumber, cut into matchsticks

2 fresh red chilies, seeded and
  finely sliced

2 tablespoons mint leaves

2 tablespoons fried shallots

COOK'S TIP

Balachan is dried shrimp or shrimp paste. It is sold in small blocks, and you will find it at Asian supermarkets.

---

1 In a blender or food processor, process the chilies, onion, balachan, lemon grass, ginger and nuts until smooth in texture.

2 Heat 3 tablespoons of the oil in a large saucepan. Add the chili paste and fry for 6 minutes. Stir in the paprika and turmeric and fry for about 2 minutes more.

3 Add the stock and the coconut milk to the pan. Bring to a boil, reduce the heat and simmer gently for 15–20 minutes. Season to taste with the fish sauce.

4 Season the seafood with salt and pepper. Heat the remaining oil in a frying pan, add the seafood and stir-fry quickly for 2–3 minutes until cooked.

5 Add the noodles to the broth and heat through. Divide among individual serving bowls. Place the fried seafood on top, then garnish with the cucumber, chilies, mint and fried shallots. Serve with the limes.

Sweet-and-sour Shrimp with Egg Noodles

A quick and easy dish full of flavor.

INGREDIENTS

Serves 4–6

½ ounce dried porcini mushrooms

1¼ cups hot water

bunch of scallions, cut into thick diagonal
　slices

1-inch piece fresh ginger, peeled and
　grated

1 red bell pepper, seeded and diced

1 can (8 ounces) water chestnuts, sliced

3 tablespoons light soy sauce

2 tablespoons sherry

12 ounces large cooked shrimp, peeled

8 ounces Chinese egg noodles

1 Put the dried porcini
mushrooms into a bowl with
the hot water and set aside to soak
for 15 minutes.

2 Put the sliced scallions,
grated ginger and diced red
pepper into a pan with the
mushrooms and their liquid. Bring
to a boil, cover and cook for about
5 minutes, until tender.

3 Add the water chestnuts, soy
sauce, sherry and shrimp.
Cover and cook gently over low
heat for 2 minutes.

4 Cook the egg noodles
according to the instructions
on the package. Drain thoroughly
and transfer to a warmed serving
dish. Spoon the hot shrimp on top.
Serve immediately.

Farfalle with Shrimp

Creamy sauces are not invariably the best way to serve fish with pasta. This simple, fresh shrimp sauce allows the distinctive flavor of the fish to be identified.

Serves 4

8 ounces fresh or dried farfalle
  (pasta bows)

12 ounces raw or cooked shrimp

8 tablespoons (1 stick) unsalted butter

2 garlic cloves, crushed

3 tablespoons chopped fresh parsley

salt and freshly ground black pepper

1 Cook fresh pasta in boiling salted water for 2–3 minutes, or until tender but still firm to the bite. Cook dried pasta according to the package instructions. Peel and devein the shrimp.

2 Heat the butter in a large heavy saucepan with the garlic and parsley. Toss in the shrimp and sauté for 8 minutes (for cooked shrimp, 4 minutes will be sufficient).

3 Drain the pasta thoroughly and rinse with boiling water to remove any starch.

4 Stir the pasta into the shrimp mixture. Season with salt and pepper to taste and serve.

Bamie Goreng

*This fried noodle dish from
Indonesia is wonderfully
accommodating. To the basic recipe
you can add other vegetables, such
as mushrooms, broccoli, leeks or
bean sprouts. You can use whatever
you have on hand, bearing in mind
the importance of achieving a
balance of colors, flavors and
textures.*

INGREDIENTS

Serves 6–8

1 pound dried egg noodles

1 boneless skinless chicken breast

4 ounces pork fillet

4 ounces calves' liver (optional)

2 eggs, beaten

6 tablespoons oil

2 tablespoons butter or margarine

2 garlic cloves, crushed

4 ounces cooked peeled large shrimp

4 ounces spinach

2 celery stalks, finely sliced

4 scallions, shredded

about ¼ cup chicken stock

dark soy sauce and light soy sauce

salt and freshly ground black pepper

deep-fried onions and celery leaves,
    to garnish

mixed fruit and vegetable salad, to
    serve (optional)

1 Cook the noodles in lightly
salted boiling water for
3–4 minutes. Drain, rinse with
cold water and drain well again.
Set aside until needed.

2 Finely slice the chicken, pork
fillet and calves' liver, if using.

3 Season the eggs. Heat
1 teaspoon of the oil with the
butter in a small pan until melted.
Stir in the eggs and keep stirring
until scrambled. Set aside.

4 Heat the remaining oil in a
preheated wok and stir-fry
the garlic with the chicken, pork
and liver for 2–3 minutes, until
they have changed color. Stir in
the shrimp, spinach, celery and
scallions, and mix well.

5 Add the drained noodles and
toss the mixture well so that
all the ingredients are thoroughly
combined. Add just enough stock
to moisten and add dark and light
soy sauce to taste. Finally, stir in
the scrambled eggs.

6 Garnish the dish with deep-
fried onions and celery leaves.
Serve with a mixed fruit and
vegetable salad, if desired.

Buckwheat Noodles with Smoked Trout

The light, crisp texture of the bok choy balances the strong, earthy flavors of the mushrooms and the smokiness of the trout.

INGREDIENTS

Serves 4

12 ounces buckwheat noodles

2 tablespoons vegetable oil

4 ounces fresh shiitake mushrooms, quartered

2 garlic cloves, finely chopped

1 tablespoon grated fresh ginger

8 ounces bok choy

1 scallion, finely sliced diagonally

1 tablespoon dark sesame oil

2 tablespoons mirin

2 tablespoons soy sauce

2 smoked trout, skinned and boned

salt and freshly ground black pepper

2 tablespoons cilantro leaves and
    2 teaspoons sesame seeds, toasted, to
    garnish

1 Cook the buckwheat noodles in a saucepan of boiling water for 7–10 minutes, or until just tender, according to the instructions on the package.

2 Meanwhile, heat the oil in a large frying pan. Add the shiitake mushrooms and sauté over medium heat for 3 minutes. Add the garlic, ginger and bok choy, and continue to sauté for another 2 minutes.

3 Drain the noodles and add them to the mushroom mixture, with the scallion, sesame oil, mirin and soy sauce. Toss and season with salt and pepper to taste.

4 Break up the trout into bite-size pieces. Arrange the noodle mixture on individual serving plates and top with trout.

5 Garnish the noodles with cilantro leaves and sesame seeds and serve immediately.

COOK'S TIP

Mirin is sweet, cooking sake, available at Japanese stores.

Stir-fried Noodles with Sweet Salmon

A delicious sauce forms the marinade for the salmon in this recipe. Served with soft-fried noodles, it makes a stunning dish.

Serves 4

12 ounces salmon fillet

2 tablespoons Japanese soy sauce (shoyu)

2 tablespoons sake

¼ cup mirin or sweet sherry

1 teaspoon light brown sugar

2 teaspoons grated fresh ginger

3 cloves garlic, 1 crushed, and 2 sliced

2 tablespoons peanut oil

8 ounces dried egg noodles, cooked and drained

2 ounces alfalfa sprouts

2 tablespoons sesame seeds, lightly toasted

1 Thinly slice the salmon, then place in a shallow dish.

2 In a bowl, combine the soy sauce, sake, mirin, sugar, ginger and crushed garlic. Pour the sauce over the salmon, cover and let marinate for 30 minutes.

3 Drain the salmon, scraping off and reserving the marinade. Place the salmon in a single layer on a baking sheet. Cook under a preheated broiler for 2–3 minutes, without turning.

4 Meanwhile, heat a wok until hot, add the oil and swirl it around. Add the garlic rounds and cook until golden brown, but do not let them burn.

5 Add the cooked noodles and reserved marinade to the wok. Stir-fry for 3–4 minutes, until the marinade has reduced slightly to make a syrupy glaze that coats the egg noodles.

6 Toss in the alfalfa sprouts, then remove immediately from the heat. Transfer to warmed serving plates and top with the salmon. Sprinkle on the toasted sesame seeds. Serve immediately.

COOK'S TIP

It is important to scrape the marinade off the fish, as any remaining pieces of ginger or garlic would burn during grilling and spoil the finished dish.

Smoked Trout Cannelloni

Smoked trout can be bought already filleted or as whole fish. They make a delicious change from the tomato-based fillings usually found in cannelloni dishes.

INGREDIENTS

Serves 4-6

1 large onion, finely chopped

1 garlic clove, crushed

¼ cup vegetable stock

2 cans (14 ounces each) chopped tomatoes

½ teaspoon dried mixed herbs

1 smoked trout, about 8 ounces

¾ cup frozen peas, thawed

½ cup fresh bread crumbs

16 cannelloni tubes, cooked

salt and freshly ground black pepper

mixed salad, to serve

For the cheese sauce

2 tablespoons butter or margarine

1 tablespoon flour

1½ cups skim milk

freshly grated nutmeg

1½ tablespoons freshly grated
    Parmesan cheese

1 Simmer the onion, garlic clove and stock in a large, covered saucepan for 3 minutes. Uncover and continue to cook, stirring occasionally, until the stock has reduced entirely.

2 Stir in the tomatoes and dried herbs. Simmer uncovered for another 10 minutes or until the mixture is very thick.

3 Meanwhile, skin the smoked trout with a sharp knife. Carefully flake the flesh and discard all the bones. Combine the fish with the tomato mixture, peas, bread crumbs, salt and freshly ground black pepper.

4 Spoon the filling into the cannelloni tubes and arrange in an ovenproof dish.

5 For the sauce, put the butter, flour and milk into a saucepan and cook over medium heat, whisking constantly, until the sauce thickens. Simmer for 2–3 minutes, stirring all the time. Season to taste with salt, freshly ground black pepper and the grated nutmeg.

6 Pour the sauce over the stuffed cannelloni and sprinkle with the grated Parmesan cheese. Bake in a preheated oven at 375°F for 30–45 minutes or until the top is golden and bubbling and the sauce is cooked through. Serve with a mixed salad.

COOK'S TIP

༄

You can use a can (7 ounces) of tuna in water instead of the trout, if preferred.

Tuna Lasagne

Lasagne does not always have to be made with ground beef.

INGREDIENTS

Serves 6

12 ounces oven-ready lasagne

1 tablespoon butter

1 small onion, finely chopped

1 garlic clove, finely chopped

4 ounces mushrooms, thinly sliced

¼ cup dry white wine (optional)

2½ cups white sauce

⅔ cup heavy cream

3 tablespoons chopped fresh parsley

2 cans (7 ounces each) tuna, drained

2 canned pimientos, cut into strips

1 cup frozen peas, thawed

4 ounces mozzarella, grated

1 ounce freshly grated Parmesan cheese

salt and freshly ground black pepper

1 Soak the sheets of lasagne in a bowl of hot water for 3–5 minutes, or prepare according to the package instructions. Drain and rinse with cold water. Lay them on a dish towel, in a single layer, to drain.

2 Melt the butter in a saucepan and gently fry the onion for 2–3 minutes, until soft but not colored. Add the garlic and mushrooms and cook until they are soft, stirring occasionally.

3 Pour in the wine, if using. Boil for 1 minute. Add the white sauce, cream and parsley and season to taste.

4 Spoon a thin layer of sauce over the base of a 12 x 9-inch baking dish. Cover with a layer of lasagne sheets. Flake the tuna. Scatter half of the tuna, pimiento strips, peas and grated mozzarella over the pasta. Spoon one-third of the remaining sauce evenly over the top and cover with another layer of lasagne sheets.

5 Repeat the layers, ending with lasagne and sauce. Sprinkle with the Parmesan. Bake in a preheated oven at 350°F for 30–40 minutes, or until bubbling hot and the top is lightly browned. Cut into squares and serve from the baking dish.

Seafood Chow Mein

This basic recipe can be adapted using a range of different items for the "'dressing."

Serves 4

3 ounces squid, cleaned

3 ounces raw shrimp

3–4 fresh scallops, prepared

½ egg white

1 tablespoon cornstarch paste

8 ounces egg noodles

5–6 tablespoons vegetable oil

2 ounces snow peas

½ teaspoon salt

½ teaspoon light brown sugar

1 tablespoon Chinese rice wine or
    dry sherry

2 tablespoons light soy sauce

2 scallions, finely shredded

vegetable or chicken stock, if necessary

few drops sesame oil

1 Open up the squid and, using a sharp knife, score the inside in a crisscross pattern. Cut the squid into pieces, each about the size of a postage stamp. Soak the squid in a bowl of boiling water until all the pieces curl up. Rinse in cold water and drain.

2 Peel and devein the shrimp, then cut each of them in half lengthwise.

3 Cut each scallop into 3–4 slices. Mix the scallops and shrimp with the egg white and cornstarch paste and set aside.

4 Cook the noodles in boiling water according to the package instructions, then drain and rinse under cold water. Mix with about 1 tablespoon of the oil.

COOK'S TIP

To make cornstarch paste, mix 4 parts dry cornstarch with about 5 parts cold water until smooth.

5 Heat 2–3 tablespoons of the oil in a preheated wok until hot. Stir-fry the snow peas and seafood for about 2 minutes, then add the salt, sugar, rice wine or sherry, half of the soy sauce and about half of the scallions. Blend well and add a little stock, if necessary. Remove and keep warm.

6 Heat the remaining oil in the wok and stir-fry the noodles for 2–3 minutes with the remaining soy sauce. Place in a large serving dish, pour the "dressing" on top, garnish with the remaining scallions and sprinkle with sesame oil. Serve hot or cold.

Seafood Rice

This tasty paella-type meal uses a frozen fish mixture that saves lots of preparation time.

Serves 4

2 tablespoons oil

1 onion, sliced

1 red bell pepper, seeded and chopped

4 ounces mushrooms, chopped

2 teaspoons ground turmeric

8 ounces arborio rice

3 cups chicken or vegetable stock

1 bag (14 ounces) frozen premium
    seafood selection, thawed

4 ounces frozen large tiger shrimp,
    thawed, peeled and deveined

salt and freshly ground black pepper

1 Heat the oil in a deep frying pan and fry the onion until it is starting to soften. Add the chopped pepper and mushrooms and fry for 1 minute.

2 Stir in the turmeric and then the rice. Stir until well mixed, then carefully pour on the stock. Season with salt and pepper, cover with a lid and let simmer gently for 15 minutes.

3 Add the seafood selection and the shrimp, stir well and turn up the heat slightly to bring the liquid back to a boil. Cover again and simmer for 15–20 more minutes, until the grains are cooked and the fish is hot. Serve the fish immediately.

COOK'S TIP

If you don't like this fish mixture, choose your own—use more shrimp and crab sticks, if you prefer, but cut down on the cooking time for the fish.

Fish with Rice

This Arabic fish dish, Sayadieh, is very popular in the Lebanon.

Serves 4–6

juice of 1 lemon

3 tablespoons oil

2 pounds cod steaks

4 large onions, chopped

1 teaspoon ground cumin

2–3 saffron strands, soaked in
  2 tablespoons hot water

4 cups fish stock

1¼ pounds basmati or long grain rice

4 ounces pine nuts, lightly toasted

salt and freshly ground black pepper

fresh parsley, to garnish

1 Combine the lemon juice and 1 tablespoon of the oil in a shallow dish. Add the fish steaks, turning to coat, then cover and set aside to marinate for 30 minutes.

2 Heat the remaining oil in a large saucepan or flameproof casserole and fry the onions for 5–6 minutes, until softened and golden, stirring occasionally.

3 Drain the fish, reserving the marinade, and add to the pan. Fry for 1–2 minutes on each side until lightly golden, then add the cumin, saffron strands and a little salt and pepper.

4 Pour in the fish stock and the reserved marinade, bring to a boil and then simmer very gently, over low heat, for 5–10 minutes, until the fish is nearly done.

5 Transfer the fish to a plate and add the rice to the stock. Bring to a boil, then reduce the heat and simmer very gently over low heat for 15 minutes, until nearly all the stock has been absorbed.

6 Arrange the fish on the rice and cover. Steam over low heat for another 15–20 minutes.

7 Transfer the fish to a plate, then spoon the rice onto a large flat dish and arrange the fish on top. Sprinkle with lightly toasted pine nuts and garnish with fresh parsley.

COOK'S TIP

Take care when cooking the rice that the saucepan does not boil dry. Check it occasionally and add more stock or water, if it becomes necessary.

Salmon Risotto

Any rice can be used for risotto, although the creamiest ones are made with short grain arborio rice. Fresh tarragon and cucumber combine well to bring out the flavor of the salmon.

Serves 4

2 tablespoons butter

1 small bunch scallions, white part only, chopped

½ cucumber, peeled, seeded and chopped

14 ounces short grain arborio rice

4 cups chicken or fish stock

⅔ cup dry white wine

1 pound salmon fillet, skinned and diced

3 tablespoons chopped fresh tarragon

1 Heat the butter in a large saucepan and add the scallions and cucumber. Cook for 2–3 minutes without coloring.

2 Add the rice, chicken stock and wine, bring to a boil and simmer, uncovered, for 10 minutes, stirring occasionally.

3 Stir in the diced salmon and chopped tarragon. Continue cooking for another 5 minutes, then switch off the heat. Cover the pan and let stand for 5 minutes before serving.

VARIATION

Long grain rice can also be used. Choose grains that have not been precooked and reduce the stock to 3 cups per 14 ounces of rice.

Truffle and Lobster Risotto

To capture the precious qualities of the fresh truffle, partner it with lobster and serve in a silky smooth arborio. Both truffle shavings and truffle oil are added toward the end of cooking to preserve their flavor.

INGREDIENTS

Serves 4

4 tablespoons (½ stick) unsalted butter

1 medium onion, chopped

14 ounces arborio or carnaroli rice

1 sprig thyme

5 cups chicken stock

⅔ cup dry white wine

1 freshly cooked lobster

3 tablespoons chopped fresh parsley and chervil

3–4 drops truffle oil

2 hard-cooked eggs, shelled and sliced

1 fresh black or white truffle, shaved

3 Remove the rice from the heat, stir in the chopped lobster meat, herbs and truffle oil. Cover and let stand for 5 minutes.

4 Divide among warmed dishes and arrange the lobster and hard-cooked egg slices and truffle shavings on top. Serve immediately.

1 Melt the butter in a large shallow pan, add the onion and fry gently until soft without letting it color. Add the rice and thyme and stir well to coat evenly with butter. Pour in the chicken stock and wine, stir once and cook, uncovered, for 15 minutes.

2 Twist off the lobster tail, cut open the underside with scissors and remove the white tail meat. Slice half of the meat, then roughly chop the remainder. Break open the claws with a small hammer and remove the flesh, in one piece if possible.

Rice Layered with Shrimp

This dish makes a meal in itself, requiring only pickles or raita as an accompaniment.

Serves 4–6

2 large onions, finely sliced and deep-fried

1¼ cups plain yogurt

1½ tablespoons tomato paste

¼ cup green masala paste

1½ tablespoons lemon juice

1 teaspoon black cumin seeds

2-inch piece cinnamon stick or
    ¼ teaspoon cinnamon

4 green cardamom pods

1 pound cooked jumbo shrimp, peeled
    and deveined

8 ounces small button mushrooms

1 cup frozen peas, thawed and drained

1 pound basmati rice, soaked for
    5 minutes in boiled water and drained

1¼ cups water

1 envelope saffron powder mixed in
    6 tablespoons milk

2 tablespoons ghee or unsalted butter

salt

1 Combine the first 8 ingredients in a large bowl. Fold in the shrimp, mushrooms and peas. Let marinate for 2 hours in the refrigerator.

2 Grease the base of a heavy pan and add the shrimp, vegetables and any marinade juices. Cover with the drained rice and smooth the surface gently until you have an even layer.

3 Pour the water all over the surface of the rice. Make random holes through the rice with the handle of a spoon and pour a little saffron milk into each.

4 Place a few pats of ghee on the surface and place a circular piece of foil directly on top of the rice. Cover and cook over low heat for 45–50 minutes. Gently toss the rice, shrimp and vegetables together and serve hot.

Spanish Seafood Paella

Paella is also the name of the heavy, cast-iron pan in which this dish is traditionally cooked.

INGREDIENTS

Serves 4

¼ cup olive oil

8 ounces monkfish or cod, skinned and cut into chunks

3 prepared baby squid, bodies cut into rings and tentacles chopped

1 red mullet, filleted, skinned and cut into chunks (optional)

1 onion, chopped

3 garlic cloves, finely chopped

1 red bell pepper, seeded and sliced

4 tomatoes, skinned and chopped

8 ounces arborio rice

2 cups fish stock

⅔ cup white wine

½ cup frozen peas

4–5 saffron strands soaked in 2 tablespoons hot water

4 ounces cooked peeled shrimp

8 fresh mussels in shells, scrubbed

salt and freshly ground black pepper

1 tablespoon chopped fresh parsley, to garnish

lemon wedges, to serve

1 Heat 2 tablespoons of the olive oil in a large frying pan and add the monkfish, the squid and the red mullet, if using. Stir-fry for 2 minutes, then transfer the fish to a bowl with all the juices and set aside.

2 Heat the remaining 2 tablespoons of oil in the pan and add the onion, garlic and red pepper. Fry for 6–7 minutes, stirring frequently, until the onion and pepper have softened.

3 Stir in the tomatoes and fry for 2 minutes, then add the rice, stirring to coat the grains with oil, and cook for 2–3 minutes. Pour on the fish stock and wine and add the peas, saffron and water. Season well and mix.

4 Gently stir in the fish with all the juices, followed by the shrimp, and then push the mussels into the rice. Cover and cook over low heat for about 30 minutes, or until the stock has been absorbed but the mixture is still moist.

5 Remove from the heat, keep covered and let stand for 5 minutes. Discard any mussels that do not open. Sprinkle the paella with parsley and serve with lemon wedges.

Smoked Trout Pilaf

Smoked trout might seem an unusual partner for rice, but this is a winning combination.

INGREDIENTS

Serves 4

8 ounces white basmati rice

3 tablespoons butter

2 onions, sliced into rings

1 garlic clove, crushed

2 bay leaves

2 cloves

2 green cardamom pods

2 cinnamon sticks

1 teaspoon cumin seeds

2½ cups boiling water

4 smoked trout fillets, skinned

¼ cup sliced almonds, toasted

¼ cup seedless raisins

2 tablespoons chopped fresh parsley

mango chutney and poppadoms, to serve

1 Wash the rice thoroughly in several changes of water and drain well. Set aside. Melt the butter in a large frying pan and fry the onions until well browned, stirring frequently.

2 Add the garlic, bay leaves, cloves, cardamom pods, cinnamon sticks and cumin seeds and stir-fry for 1 minute.

3 Stir in the rice, then add the boiling water. Bring back to a boil. Cover the pan tightly, reduce the heat and cook very gently for 20–25 minutes, or until the water has been absorbed and the rice is just tender.

4 Flake the smoked trout and add to the pan with the almonds and raisins. Fork through gently. Cover the pan and let the smoked trout warm in the rice for a few minutes. Scatter on the parsley and serve with mango chutney and poppadoms.

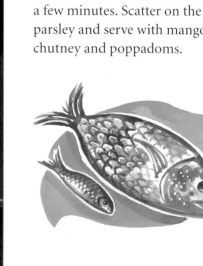

Mixed Fish Jambalaya

Jambalaya, from New Orleans, is not unlike a paella, but much spicier. The name comes from the French word "jambon," and tells us that the dish was originally based on ham, but you can add many other ingredients of your choice, including fish and shellfish.

INGREDIENTS

Serves 4

2 tablespoons oil

6–8 strips bacon, diced

1 onion, chopped

2 stalks celery, chopped

2 large garlic cloves, chopped

1 teaspoon cayenne pepper

2 bay leaves

1 teaspoon dried oregano

½ teaspoon dried thyme

4 medium tomatoes, skinned, seeded and chopped

⅔ cup ready-made tomato sauce

12 ounces long grain rice

2 cups fish stock

6 ounces firm white fish (cod or haddock), skinned, boned and cubed

4 ounces cooked peeled shrimp

salt and freshly ground black pepper

2 chopped scallions, to garnish

1 Heat the oil in a large saucepan and fry the bacon until crisp. Add the onion and celery and stir until they begin to stick to the base of the pan.

2 Add the garlic, cayenne pepper, herbs, tomatoes and seasoning and mix well. Stir in the tomato sauce, rice and stock and bring to a boil.

3 Gently stir in the fish and transfer to an ovenproof dish. Cover tightly with foil and bake at 350°F for 20–30 minutes, until the rice is just tender. Stir in the shrimp and heat through. Serve sprinkled with the scallions.

Indonesian Pork and Shrimp Rice

Nasi Goreng is an attractive way of using up leftovers and appears in many variations throughout Indonesia. Rice is the main ingredient, although almost anything can be added for color and flavor.

INGREDIENTS

Serves 4–6

3 eggs

¼ cup vegetable oil

6 shallots, or 1 large onion, chopped

2 garlic cloves, crushed

1-inch piece fresh ginger, chopped

2–3 small red chilies, seeded and
    finely chopped

1 tablespoon tamarind sauce

½-inch square piece shrimp paste or
    1 tablespoon fish sauce

½ teaspoon turmeric

2 tablespoons unsweetened cream of
    coconut

juice of 2 limes

2 teaspoons sugar

12 ounces lean pork or chicken breasts,
    skinned and sliced

12 ounces raw or cooked shrimp, peeled

1 cup bean sprouts

1 small bunch spinach, shredded

1 cup frozen peas, thawed

8 ounces long grain rice, cooked

salt

1 small bunch cilantro or basil, roughly
    chopped, to garnish

1 In a bowl, beat the eggs with a pinch of salt. Heat a non-stick frying pan over medium heat. Pour in the eggs and move the pan around until they begin to set. When set, roll up, slice thinly, cover and set aside.

2 Heat 1 tablespoon of the oil in a preheated wok and fry the shallots until evenly browned. Remove from the wok, set aside and keep warm.

3 Heat the remaining 3 tablespoons of oil in the wok, add the garlic, ginger and chilies, and soften without coloring. Stir in the tamarind and shrimp paste or fish sauce, turmeric, cream of coconut, lime juice, sugar and salt to taste. Cook briefly over medium heat, stirring constantly. Add the pork or chicken and shrimp and fry for 3–4 minutes.

4 Toss the bean sprouts, spinach and peas in the spice mixture and cook briefly. Add the rice and stir-fry for 6–8 minutes, stirring to prevent it from burning. Transfer to a large serving plate, decorate with shredded egg pancake, the fried shallots, and chopped cilantro or basil.

Mixed Smoked Fish Kedgeree

*An ideal breakfast dish on a cold
morning. Garnish with quartered
hard-cooked eggs and season well.*

INGREDIENTS

Serves 6

1 pound mixed smoked fish such as
   smoked cod, smoked haddock, smoked
   mussels or oysters if available

1¼ cups milk

6 ounces long grain rice

1 slice lemon

4 tablespoons (½ stick) butter

1 teaspoon medium curry powder

½ teaspoon freshly grated nutmeg

1 tablespoon chopped fresh parsley

salt and freshly ground black pepper

2 hard-cooked eggs, shelled and
   quartered, to serve

2 Cook the rice in salted boiling
water, together with a slice of
lemon, for 10 minutes, until just
cooked. Drain well.

3 Melt the butter in a large heavy
saucepan and add the rice and
fish. Shake the saucepan to
combine all the ingredients.

4 Stir in the curry powder,
nutmeg, parsley and
seasoning. Serve immediately,
garnished with quartered eggs.

1 Put the smoked fish and milk
in a pan, cover and poach for
10 minutes or until it flakes. Drain
off the milk and flake the fish. Mix
with the smoked seafood.

Sea Bream with Orange Sauce

Sea bream is a taste revelation to anyone not yet familiar with its creamy rich flavor. The fish has a firm white flesh that goes perfectly with a rich butter sauce, sharpened here with a dash of frozen orange juice concentrate.

INGREDIENTS

Serves 2

2 sea bream (12 ounces each), scaled and gutted

2 teaspoons Dijon mustard

1 teaspoon fennel seeds

2 tablespoons olive oil

1 small bunch watercress

6 ounces mixed salad greens, such as oak leaf lettuce or frisée

baked potatoes and orange slices, to serve

For the sauce

2 tablespoons frozen orange juice concentrate

12 tablespoons unsalted butter, diced

salt and cayenne pepper

1 Slash the bream diagonally four times on either side with a sharp knife. Combine the mustard and fennel seeds, then spread over both sides of the fish. Moisten with oil and broil for 12 minutes, turning once.

2 Place the orange juice concentrate in a bowl and heat over 1 inch of boiling water. Remove the pan from the heat and gradually whisk the butter into the juice until creamy. Season, cover and set aside.

3 Moisten the watercress and salad greens with the remaining olive oil. Arrange the fish on two large plates, spoon the sauce over them and serve with the salad greens, baked potatoes and orange slices.

COOK'S TIP

For speedy baked potatoes, microwave small potatoes on 100% high power for 8 minutes, then crisp in an oven preheated to 400°F for another 10 minutes. Split, insert butter and serve.

Monkfish with Mexican Salsa

Monkfish is a firm, meaty fish; you can use halibut or cod in its place.

INGREDIENTS

Serves 4

1½ pounds monkfish tail

3 tablespoons olive oil

2 tablespoons lime juice

1 garlic clove, crushed

1 tablespoon chopped fresh cilantro

salt and freshly ground black pepper

cilantro sprigs and lime slices, to garnish

For the salsa

4 tomatoes, skinned, seeded and diced

1 avocado, peeled, pitted and diced

½ red onion, chopped

1 green chili, seeded and chopped

2 tablespoons chopped fresh cilantro

2 tablespoons olive oil

1 tablespoon lime juice

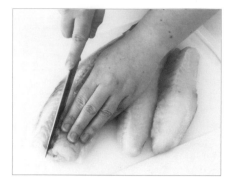

2 Prepare the monkfish. Using a sharp knife, remove the pinkish-gray membrane. Cut the fillets from either side of the backbone. Cut each fillet in half.

3 Combine the oil, lime juice, garlic, cilantro and seasoning in a non-metallic dish.

4 Add the monkfish to the dish. Turn the monkfish several times to coat with the marinade, then cover the dish and let marinate at room temperature or in the refrigerator for 30 minutes.

5 Remove the monkfish from the marinade and broil for 10–12 minutes, turning once and brushing regularly with the marinade, until cooked through.

6 Serve the monkfish garnished with fresh cilantro sprigs and lime slices and accompanied by the salsa.

1 To make the salsa, combine all the salsa ingredients and set aside at room temperature for about 40 minutes.

COOK'S TIP

It is important to remove the tough, pinkish-gray membrane covering the monkfish tail before cooking, otherwise it will shrink and toughen the monkfish.

Red Snapper with Cilantro Salsa

Snapper is a firm fish with little fat and benefits from a sauce with lots of texture and flavor.

Serves 4

4 red snapper fillets, about 6 ounces each

1½ tablespoons vegetable oil

1 tablespoon butter

salt and freshly ground black pepper

For the salsa

1 bunch fresh cilantro, stalks removed

1 cup olive oil

2 garlic cloves, chopped

2 tomatoes, seeded and chopped

2 tablespoons fresh orange juice

1 tablespoon sherry vinegar

cilantro sprigs and orange peel,
   to garnish

salad, to serve (optional)

3 Rinse the fish fillets and pat dry, then sprinkle with salt and pepper on both sides. Heat the oil and butter in a large frying pan. When hot, add the fish and cook for 2–3 minutes on each side or until opaque throughout. Cook the fish in two batches, if necessary.

4 Transfer the fillets to warmed serving plates. Top with a spoonful of salsa. Serve, garnished with cilantro and orange peel and with a salad, if desired.

1 To make the salsa, place the cilantro, oil and garlic in a food processor or blender. Process until almost smooth. Add the tomatoes and pulse on and off several times; the mixture should be slightly chunky.

2 Transfer the mixture to a bowl. Stir in the orange juice, vinegar and salt to taste, then set the salsa aside.

Fish Steaks with Mustard Sauce

This mustard sauce turns a plain fish into something special.

Serves 4-6

4–6 halibut or turbot steaks,
    1 inch thick
4 tablespoons (½ stick) butter, melted
salt and freshly ground black pepper
frisée and lemon wedges, to garnish

For the mustard sauce
¼ cup Dijon mustard
1¼ cups heavy cream
½ teaspoon superfine sugar
1 tablespoon white wine vinegar or
    lemon juice

1 Season the fish steaks with salt and pepper. Arrange them on an oiled rack in a broiler pan and brush the tops of the steaks with melted butter.

2 Broil about 4 inches from the heat, for 4–5 minutes on each side, or until cooked through. Brush with more melted butter when you turn the steaks.

3 Meanwhile, make the sauce. Combine the ingredients in a saucepan and bring to a boil, whisking constantly. Simmer, whisking, until the sauce thickens. Remove from the heat, set aside and keep warm.

4 Transfer the fish to warmed plates. Spoon on the sauce and serve immediately, garnished with frisée and lemon wedges.

Spiced Fish Baked Thai Style

Banana leaves make a perfect, natural wrapping for barbecued foods, but if they are not available, you can use foil instead.

Serves 4

4 red snapper or mullet, about
   12 ounces each
banana leaves (optional)
1 lime, plus extra slices to serve
1 garlic clove, thinly sliced
2 scallions, thinly sliced
2 tablespoons Thai red curry paste
¼ cup coconut milk

1 Clean the fish, removing the scales, and then cut several deep slashes in the sides of each with a sharp knife. Place each fish on a layer of banana leaves or foil.

2 Thinly slice half the lime and tuck the slices into the slashes in the fish, together with slivers of garlic. Scatter the scallions over the fish.

3 Grate the rind and squeeze the juice from the remaining half-lime and mix with the curry paste and coconut milk. Spoon the mixture over the fish.

4 Wrap the banana leaves or foil over the fish to enclose them completely. Tie securely with string and cook on a medium-hot barbecue for 15–20 minutes, turning occasionally. Serve with lime slices.

COOK'S TIP

A large, whole fish can also be cooked this way. A rough guide for cooking whole fish is to allow about 10 minutes per 1 inch thickness.

Trout with Almonds

This simple and quick recipe doubles easily—you can cook the trout in two frying pans or in batches. In Normandy, hazelnuts might be used in place of almonds.

INGREDIENTS

Serves 2

2 trout, about 12 ounces each, cleaned

¾ cup plain flour

4 tablespoons (½ stick) butter

¼ cup sliced almonds

2 tablespoons dry white wine

salt and freshly ground black pepper

1 Rinse the trout and pat dry. Put the flour in a large plastic bag and season with salt and pepper. Place the trout, 1 at a time, in the bag and shake to coat with flour. Shake off the excess and discard the remaining flour.

2 Melt half the butter in a large frying pan over medium heat. When it is foamy, add the trout and cook for 6–7 minutes on each side, until golden brown and the flesh next to the bone is opaque. Transfer the fish to warmed plates and keep warm.

3 Add the remaining butter to the pan and cook the almonds until just lightly browned. Add the wine to the pan and bring to a boil. Boil for 1 minute, stirring constantly, until slightly syrupy. Pour or spoon the sauce over the fish and serve immediately.

St. Rémy Tuna

St. Rémy is a beautiful village in Provence in the south of France. Herbs, such as thyme, rosemary and oregano, grow wild on the nearby hillside and feature in many of the recipes from this area.

INGREDIENTS

Serves 4

4 tuna steaks, about 6–7 ounces each,
    1 inch thick

2–3 tablespoons olive oil

3–4 garlic cloves, finely chopped

¼ cup dry white wine

3 ripe plum tomatoes, skinned, seeded
    and chopped

1 teaspoon dried **herbes de Provence**

salt and freshly ground black pepper

fresh basil leaves, to garnish

fried potatoes, to serve

1 Season the tuna steaks with salt and pepper. Set a heavy frying pan over high heat until very hot, add the oil and swirl to coat. Add the tuna steaks and press down gently, then reduce the heat to medium and cook for 6–8 minutes, turning once, until just slightly pink in the center.

2 Transfer the steaks to a serving plate and cover to keep warm.

3 Add the garlic to the pan and fry for 15–20 seconds, stirring constantly, then pour in the wine and boil until it is reduced by half. Add the tomatoes and dried herbs and cook for 2–3 minutes, until bubbling. Season with pepper and pour the sauce over the fish steaks. Garnish with fresh basil leaves and serve with fried potatoes.

COOK'S TIP

Tuna is often served pink in the middle, rather like beef. If you prefer it cooked through, reduce the heat and cook for an extra few minutes.

Donu's Lobster Piri Piri

Lobster in its shell, in true Nigerian style, flavored with dried shrimp.

INGREDIENTS

Serves 2–4

2 cooked lobsters, halved
fresh cilantro sprigs, to garnish
boiled white rice, to serve

For the piri piri sauce

¼ cup vegetable oil
2 onions, chopped
1 teaspoon chopped fresh ginger
1 pound fresh or canned
    tomatoes, chopped
1 tablespoon tomato paste
8 ounces cooked peeled shrimp
2 teaspoons ground coriander
1 green chili, seeded and chopped
1 tablespoon ground dried shrimp
    or crayfish
2½ cups water
1 green bell pepper, seeded and sliced
salt and freshly ground black pepper

3 Stir in the water, sliced green pepper and salt and pepper to taste, bring to a boil and simmer, uncovered, over medium heat for 20–30 minutes, until the sauce is reduced.

4 Add the lobsters to the sauce and cook for a few minutes to heat through. Arrange the lobster halves on warmed serving plates and pour the sauce over each one. Garnish with cilantro sprigs and serve with fluffy white rice.

1 Heat the oil in a large flame-proof casserole and fry the onions, ginger, tomatoes and tomato paste for 5 minutes or until the onions are soft.

2 Add the shrimp, ground coriander, chili and ground dried shrimp and stir well to mix.

Spicy Squid

This aromatically spiced squid dish, Cumi Cumi Smoor, is a favorite in Madura, Indonesia and is simple yet utterly delicious. Gone are the days when cleaning squid was such a chore: Now they can be bought ready-cleaned and are available at fish stores, market stalls or the freezers or fish counters of large supermarkets.

INGREDIENTS

Serves 3–4

1½ pounds squid, cleaned

3 tablespoons peanut oil

1 onion, finely chopped

2 garlic cloves, crushed

1 beefsteak tomato, skinned and chopped

1 tablespoon dark soy sauce

½ teaspoon ground nutmeg

6 cloves

⅔ cup water

juice of ½ lemon or lime

salt and freshly ground black pepper

boiled rice, to serve

1 Cut the squid bodies into ribbons and chop the tentacles. Rinse and drain well.

2 Heat a wok, toss in the squid and stir constantly for 2–3 minutes, by which time the squid will have curled into attractive shapes or firm rings. Lift out and set aside in a warm place.

3 Heat the oil in a clean pan and fry the onion and garlic, until soft and beginning to brown. Add the tomato, soy sauce, nutmeg, cloves, water and lemon or lime juice. Bring to a boil, then reduce the heat and add the squid with seasoning to taste.

4 Cook gently for another 3–5 minutes, stirring occasionally. Take care not to overcook the squid. Serve hot or warm, with boiled rice.

VARIATION

Try using 1 pound cooked peeled large shrimp in this recipe. Add them for the final 1–2 minutes.

Mackerel with Mustard and Lemon Butter

Look for bright, firm-looking, really fresh mackerel.

Serves 4

4 fresh mackerel, about 10 ounces each, gutted and cleaned
1 bunch baby spinach

For the mustard and lemon butter
8 tablespoons (1 stick) butter, melted
2 tablespoons whole-grain mustard
grated rind of 1 lemon
2 tablespoons lemon juice
3 tablespoons chopped fresh parsley
salt and freshly ground black pepper

1 To prepare each mackerel, cut off the heads just behind the gills, using a sharp knife, then cut along the belly so that the fish can be opened out flat.

2 Place the fish on a board, skin side up, and, with the heel of your hand, press along the backbone to loosen it.

3 Turn the fish the right way up and pull the bone away from the flesh. Remove the tail and cut each fish in half lengthwise. Wash and pat dry.

4 Score the skin three or four times, then season the fish. To make the mustard and lemon butter, combine the melted butter, mustard, lemon rind and juice, parsley and seasoning. Place the mackerel on a broiler pan. Brush a little of the butter on the mackerel and broil for 5 minutes on each side, basting occasionally, until cooked through.

5 Arrange the spinach leaves in the center of 4 large plates. Place the mackerel on top. Heat the remaining butter in a small pan until sizzling and pour it over the mackerel. Serve immediately.

Turkish Cold Fish

Cold fish dishes are appreciated in the Middle East and for good reason—they are delicious. This particular version from Turkey can be made using mackerel, if preferred.

INGREDIENTS

Serves 4

¼ cup olive oil

2 pounds porgy or snapper

2 onions, sliced

1 green bell pepper, seeded and sliced

1 red bell pepper, seeded and sliced

3 garlic cloves, crushed

1 tablespoon tomato paste

¼ cup fish stock, bottled clam juice or
    water

5–6 tomatoes, skinned and sliced or 1 can
    (14 ounces) tomatoes

2 tablespoons chopped fresh parsley

2 tablespoons lemon juice

1 teaspoon paprika

15–20 green and black olives

salt and freshly ground black pepper

bread and salad, to serve

1 Heat 2 tablespoons of the oil in a large roasting pan or frying pan and fry the fish on both sides until golden brown. Remove from the pan, cover and keep warm.

2 Heat the remaining oil in the pan and fry the onion for 2–3 minutes, until softened. Add the peppers and continue cooking for 3–4 minutes, stirring occasionally, then add the garlic and stir-fry for 1 more minute.

3 Blend the tomato paste with the fish stock, clam juice or water and stir into the pan with the tomatoes, parsley, lemon juice, paprika and seasoning. Simmer very gently for 15 minutes, stirring occasionally.

4 Return the fish to the pan and cover with the sauce. Cook for 10 minutes, then add the olives and cook for another 5 minutes or until just cooked through.

5 Transfer the fish to a serving dish and pour the sauce on top. Let cool, then cover and chill until completely cold. Serve cold with bread and salad.

> ### COOK'S TIP
> One large fish looks spectacular, but it is tricky both to cook and to serve. If you prefer, buy 4 smaller fish and cook for a shorter time, until just tender and cooked through.

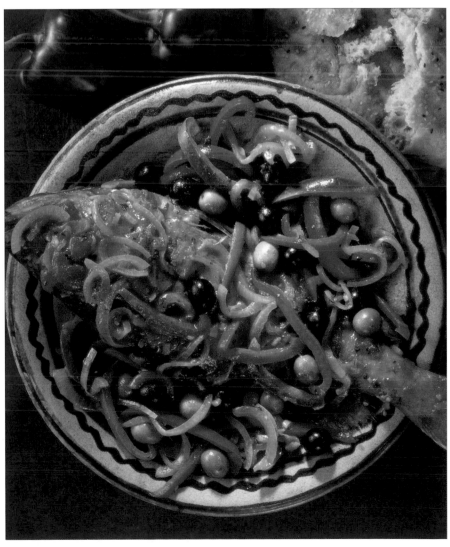

Fish Steaks with Cilantro-lime Butter

Citrus-flavored butter adds just the right kind of zip to fish steaks.

INGREDIENTS

Serves 4

1½ pounds swordfish or tuna steak, 1 inch thick, cut into 4 pieces

¼ cup vegetable oil

2 tablespoons lemon juice

1 tablespoon lime juice

salt and freshly ground black pepper

cilantro-lime butter (see Cook's Tip)

asparagus and lime slices, to serve

1 Put the fish steaks in a shallow dish. Combine the oil, lemon juice and lime juice, season and pour over the fish. Cover and refrigerate for 1–2 hours, turning the fish once or twice.

2 Drain the fish steaks and arrange on a hot broiler pan, or set over the hot charcoal about 5 inches from the coals. Grill for 3–4 minutes or until the fish is just firm to the touch but still moist in the center, turning the steaks over once.

3 Transfer to warmed plates and top each fish steak with a pat of cilantro-lime butter. Serve the fish immediately with asparagus and slices of lime.

COOK'S TIP

For cilantro-lime butter, finely chop 1 small bunch fresh cilantro. Mix into 1 stick softened, unsalted butter, together with the grated rind and juice of 1 lime. Roll the butter neatly in waxed paper and chill in the refrigerator until firm. Other flavored butters can be made in the same way. Try parsley-lemon butter, made from 2 tablespoons chopped parsley, 1 stick unsalted butter and 1 tablespoon lemon juice.

Trout in Wine Sauce with Plantain

Tropical fish would add a distinctive flavor to this Caribbean dish.

INGREDIENTS

Serves 4

1 tablespoon garlic powder

1½ teaspoons coarse-grain black pepper

1½ teaspoons paprika

1½ teaspoons celery salt

1½ teaspoons curry powder

1 teaspoon superfine sugar

4 trout fillets

2 tablespoons butter

⅔ cup white wine

⅔ cup fish stock

2 teaspoons honey

1–2 tablespoons chopped fresh parsley

1 yellow plantain

oil, for frying

1 Combine the spices and the superfine sugar, sprinkle over the trout and marinate for 1 hour.

2 Melt the butter in a frying pan and sauté the fillets for about 5 minutes, until cooked through, turning once. Transfer to a plate and keep warm.

3 Add the wine, fish stock and honey to the pan, bring to a boil and simmer to reduce slightly. Return the fillets to the pan and spoon on the sauce. Sprinkle with parsley and simmer gently for a few minutes.

4 Meanwhile, peel the plantain, and cut into rounds. Heat a little oil in a frying pan and fry the plantain until golden, turning once. Transfer the fish to warmed serving plates, stir the sauce and pour it over the fish. Garnish with the fried plantain.

Salmon Cakes with Spicy Mayonnaise

Taste the difference between home-made fish cakes and the inferior store-bought variety with this delicious recipe.

INGREDIENTS

Serves 4

2 boiling potatoes, about 12 ounces

12 ounces salmon fillet, skinned and
  finely chopped

2–3 tablespoons chopped fresh dill

1 tablespoon lemon juice

flour, for coating

3 tablespoons vegetable oil

salt and freshly ground black pepper

spicy mayonnaise (see Cook's Tip) and
  salad greens, to serve

1 Put the potatoes in a saucepan of boiling salted water and parboil them for 15 minutes.

2 Meanwhile, combine the salmon, dill, lemon juice, salt and pepper in a large bowl.

3 Drain the potatoes and let them cool. When they are cool enough to handle, peel away the skins.

4 Shred the potatoes into strips on the coarse side of a grater.

5 Add to the salmon mixture. Combine gently with your fingers, breaking up the strips of potato as little as possible.

6 Divide the salmon and potato mixture into 8 portions. Shape each into a compact cake, pressing well together. Flatten the cakes to about ½ inch thickness.

7 Coat the salmon cakes lightly with flour, shaking off excess.

8 Heat the oil in a large frying pan. Add the salmon cakes and fry for 5 minutes or until crisp and golden brown on both sides.

9 Drain the salmon cakes on paper towels and serve with the spicy mayonnaise and salad.

COOK'S TIP

To make spicy mayonnaise, combine 1½ cups mayonnaise, 2 teaspoons Dijon mustard, ½–1 teaspoon Worcestershire sauce and a dash of Tabasco sauce. You can use home-made or good quality commercial mayonnaise.

Tuna and Corn Fish Cakes

These economical little tuna fish cakes are quick to make. Use fresh mashed potatoes or make a quick version with instant mashed potatoes.

INGREDIENTS

Serves 4

2 cups cooked mashed potatoes

1 can (7 ounces) tuna fish in soy oil, drained and flaked

¾ cup canned corn

2 tablespoons chopped fresh parsley

½ cup fresh white or brown bread crumbs

salt and freshly ground black pepper

lemon wedges, to garnish

fresh vegetables, to serve

1 Place the mashed potatoes in a bowl and stir in the tuna fish, corn and chopped parsley.

2 Season to taste with salt and pepper, then shape into 8 patty shapes with your hands.

3 Spread out the bread crumbs on a plate and gently press the fish cakes into the bread crumbs to coat lightly, then transfer to a baking sheet.

4 Cook the fish cakes under a moderately hot broiler until crisp and golden brown, turning once. Serve hot with the lemon wedges and fresh vegetables.

COOK'S TIP

For simple variations, which are just as nutritious, try using canned sardines, red or pink salmon, or smoked mackerel in place of the tuna fish.

Fresh Tuna Teriyaki

Teriyaki is a sweet soy marinade usually used to glaze meat. Here it enhances fresh tuna steaks served with rich shiitake mushrooms.

INGREDIENTS

Serves 4

4 fresh tuna or yellowfin tail steaks
  (6 ounces each)
6 ounces shiitake mushrooms, sliced
⅔ cup teriyaki sauce
8 ounces white radish, peeled
2 large carrots, peeled
salt
boiled rice, to serve

1 Season the tuna steaks with a sprinkling of salt, then set aside for 20 minutes for it to penetrate. Combine the fish and sliced mushrooms, pour the teriyaki sauce over them and set aside to marinate for another 20–30 minutes or longer if you have the time.

COOK'S TIP

You can make your own teriyaki sauce by combining 6 table-spoons shoyu, 1 tablespoon superfine sugar, 1 tablespoon dry white wine and 1 tablespoon rice wine or dry sherry.

2 Drain the tuna, reserving the marinade and mushrooms. Broil the tuna or grill on a barbecue for about 8 minutes, turning once.

3 Transfer the mushrooms and marinade to a stainless steel saucepan and simmer over medium heat for 3–4 minutes.

4 Slice the radish and carrots thinly, then shred finely with a chopping knife. Arrange in heaps on 4 serving plates and add the fish, with the mushrooms and sauce poured on top. Serve with plain boiled rice.

Whiting Fillets in a Polenta Crust

Polenta is sometimes called cornmeal. Use instant polenta if you can, as it will give a better crunchy coating.

INGREDIENTS

Serves 4

8 small whiting fillets

finely grated rind of 1 lemon

8 ounces polenta

2 tablespoons olive oil

1 tablespoon butter

2 tablespoons mixed fresh herbs, such as
    parsley, chervil and chives

salt and freshly ground black pepper

toasted pine nuts and red onion, sliced,
    to garnish

steamed spinach, to serve

1 Make 4 small cuts in each fillet to prevent the fish from curling up when it is cooked.

2 Sprinkle the seasoning and lemon rind over the fish.

3 Press the polenta onto the fillets. Chill in the refrigerator for 30 minutes.

4 Heat the oil and butter in a large frying pan and gently fry the fillets on each side for 3–4 minutes. Sprinkle on the fresh herbs and garnish with toasted pine nuts and red onion slices. Serve with steamed spinach.

Herrings in Oatmeal with Mustard

Oatmeal makes a delicious, crunchy coating for tender herrings.

INGREDIENTS

Serves 4

1 tablespoon Dijon mustard

1½ teaspoons tarragon vinegar

¾ cup thick mayonnaise

4 herrings, about 8 ounces each, gutted
 and cleaned

1 lemon, halved

1½ cups oatmeal

salt and freshly ground black pepper

1 Beat mustard and vinegar to taste into the mayonnaise. Chill lightly.

2 Place one fish at a time on a board, cut side down and opened out. Press gently along the backbone with your thumbs. Turn over the fish and carefully lift away the backbone.

3 Squeeze lemon juice over both sides of the fish, then season with salt and pepper. Fold the fish in half, skin side outward.

4 Place the oatmeal on a plate, then coat each herring evenly in the oatmeal, pressing it in gently but firmly.

5 Place the herrings on a broiler pan and broil for 3–4 minutes on each side, until the skin is golden brown and crisp and the flesh flakes easily. Serve immediately with the mustard sauce, served separately.

Fish and Chips

This classic British dish is quick and easy to make at home.

INGREDIENTS

Serves 4

1 cup self-rising flour

⅔ cup water

1½ pounds potatoes

oil, for deep-frying

1½-pound piece skinned cod fillet, cut
 into 4 pieces

salt

lemon wedges, to garnish

1 Sift the flour and a pinch of salt together in a bowl, then form a well in the center. Gradually pour in the water, whisking in the flour to make a smooth batter. Set aside to rest for 30 minutes.

2 Cut the potatoes into strips about ½ inch wide and 2 inches long. Place them in a colander and rinse in cold water, then drain and dry well.

3 Heat the oil in a deep-fat fryer or large heavy pan to 300°F. Using the wire basket, lower the potatoes in batches into the oil and cook for 5–6 minutes, shaking the basket occasionally, until the potatoes are soft but not browned. Remove the chips from the oil and drain thoroughly on paper towels.

4 Heat the oil in the fryer to 375°F. Season the fish. Stir the batter, then dip the pieces of fish into it, in turn, letting the excess drain off.

5 Working in two batches if necessary, lower the fish into the oil and fry for 6–8 minutes, until crisp and golden brown. Drain the fish on paper towels and keep warm.

6 Add the chips in batches to the oil and cook for 2–3 minutes, until golden brown and crisp. Keep hot. Sprinkle with salt and serve with the fish, garnished with lemon wedges.

Cod with Caper Sauce

This quick and easy sauce, with a slightly sharp and nutty flavor, is a very effective way of enhancing a rather bland fish.

INGREDIENTS

Serves 4

4 cod steaks, about 6 ounces each
8 tablespoons (1 stick) butter
1 tablespoon vinegar
1 tablespoon capers
1 tablespoon chopped fresh parsley
salt and freshly ground black pepper
tarragon sprigs, to garnish

1 Season the cod with salt and pepper. Melt 2 tablespoons of the butter, then brush some over one side of each piece of cod.

2 Cook the cod in a preheated oven for about 6 minutes, turn it over, brush with more melted butter and cook for another 5–6 minutes or until the fish flakes easily.

3 Meanwhile, heat the remaining butter until it turns golden brown, but do not let it burn. Add the vinegar, followed by the capers, and stir well.

4 Pour the vinegar, butter and capers over the fish, sprinkle with parsley and garnish with the tarragon sprigs.

COOK'S TIP

Thick tail fillets of cod or haddock could be used in place of the cod steaks, if desired.

Cod with Spiced Red Lentils

This delicious dish marries the spices of India with the delicate flavor of cod.

INGREDIENTS

Serves 4

6 ounces red lentils

¼ teaspoon ground turmeric

2½ cups fish stock

2 tablespoons vegetable oil

1½ teaspoons cumin seeds

1 tablespoon grated fresh ginger

½ teaspoon cayenne pepper

1 tablespoon lemon juice

2 tablespoons chopped fresh cilantro

1 pound cod fillets, skinned and cut into
   large chunks

salt

cilantro leaves and 4–8 lemon wedges,
   to garnish

1 Put the lentils in a pan with the turmeric and stock. Bring to a boil, cover and simmer for 20–25 minutes, until the lentils are just tender. Remove from the heat and add salt to taste.

2 Heat the oil in a small frying pan. Add the cumin seeds and, when they begin to pop, add the ginger and cayenne pepper. Stir-fry the spices for a few seconds, then pour onto the lentils. Add the lemon juice and the chopped cilantro and stir in gently.

3 Lay the pieces of cod on top of the lentils, cover the pan and then cook gently over low heat for 10–15 minutes, until the fish is tender and flaky.

4 Transfer the lentils and cod to warmed serving plates. Sprinkle on the cilantro leaves and garnish each serving with 1–2 lemon wedges. Serve hot.

Fish Fillets with Orange and Tomato Sauce

Citrus flavors liven up any plain white fish beautifully.

Serves 4

3 tablespoons flour

4 fillets of firm white fish, such as cod, sea bass or sole, about 1½ pounds

1 tablespoon butter or margarine

2 tablespoons olive oil

1 onion, sliced

2 garlic cloves, chopped

¼ teaspoon ground cumin

1¼ pounds tomatoes, skinned, seeded and chopped, or 1 can (14 ounces) chopped tomatoes

½ cup fresh orange juice

salt and freshly ground black pepper

orange wedges, for garnishing

1 Put the flour on a plate and season well with salt and pepper. Coat the fish fillets lightly with the seasoned flour, shaking off any excess.

2 Heat the butter and half the oil in a large frying pan. Add the fish fillets to the pan and cook for about 3 minutes on each side, until golden brown and the flesh flakes easily when tested with a fork.

3 When the fish is cooked, transfer to a warmed serving platter. Cover with foil and keep warm while you make the sauce.

4 Heat the remaining oil in the pan. Add the onion and garlic and cook for about 5 minutes, until softened but not colored.

5 Stir in the ground cumin, tomatoes and orange juice. Bring to a boil and cook, stirring frequently, for about 10 minutes, until thickened.

6 Garnish the fish with orange wedges and serve immediately, passing the sauce separately.

Cajun-style Cod

This recipe works equally well with any firm-fleshed fish, such as swordfish, shark, tuna or halibut.

INGREDIENTS

Serves 4

4 cod steaks, each weighing about
  6 ounces
2 tablespoons plain yogurt
1 tablespoon lime or lemon juice
1 garlic clove, crushed
1 teaspoon ground cumin
1 teaspoon paprika
1 teaspoon mustard powder
½ teaspoon cayenne powder
½ teaspoon dried thyme
½ teaspoon oregano
vegetable oil, for brushing
new potatoes and mixed greens,
  to serve

1 Pat the fish dry on absorbent paper towels. Combine the yogurt and lime juice and brush lightly over both sides of the fish.

2 Combine the garlic, cumin, paprika, mustard powder, cayenne, thyme and oregano. Coat both sides of the fish with the seasoning mix, rubbing in well.

3 Brush a ridged grill pan or heavy frying pan with a little oil. Heat until very hot. Add the fish and cook over high heat for 4 minutes or until the underside is well browned.

4 Brush the fish with a little more oil, if necessary, turn over and cook for another 4 minutes or until the steaks have cooked through. Serve immediately, accompanied with new potatoes and mixed greens.

Monkfish with Peppered Citrus Marinade

Monkfish is a firm, meaty fish that cooks well on the barbecue and keeps its shape.

INGREDIENTS

Serves 4

2 monkfish tails, about 12 ounces each

1 lime

1 lemon

2 oranges

handful of fresh thyme sprigs

2 tablespoons olive oil

1 tablespoon mixed peppercorns, roughly crushed

salt and freshly ground black pepper

lemon and lime wedges, to serve

3 Cut 2 slices each from the lime, lemon and 1 orange and arrange them over 2 of the fillets. Add a few sprigs of thyme and sprinkle with salt and pepper. Finely grate the rind from the remaining fruit and sprinkle it over the fish.

5 Squeeze the juice from the remaining lime, lemon and oranges and mix it with the oil and more salt and pepper to taste. Spoon over the fish. Cover and let marinate for about 1 hour, turning occasionally and spooning the marinade over it.

1 Remove any skin from the monkfish tails. Cut carefully down one side of the backbone, sliding the knife between the bone and flesh, to remove the fillet on one side. You can ask your fishmonger to do this for you.

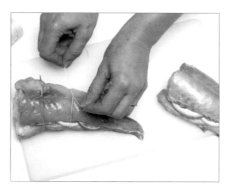

4 Lay the remaining 2 fish fillets on top and tie them firmly with fine cotton string to hold them in shape. Arrange them in a wide dish.

6 Drain the monkfish, reserving the marinade, and sprinkle with the crushed peppercorns. Cook on a medium-hot barbecue for 15–20 minutes, basting it with the marinade and turning it occasionally, until it is evenly cooked through. Serve with lemon and lime wedges.

VARIATION

You can also use this marinade for monkfish kebabs.

2 Turn the fish and repeat on the other side, to remove the second fillet. Repeat on the second tail. Lay the 4 fillets out flat.

Haddock with Parsley Sauce

As the fish has to be kept warm while the sauce is being made, take care not to overcook it.

Serves 4

4 haddock fillets, about 6 ounces each

4 tablespoons (½ stick) butter

⅔ cup milk

⅔ cup fish stock

1 bay leaf

4 teaspoons flour

¼ cup heavy cream

1 egg yolk

3 tablespoons chopped fresh parsley

grated rind and juice of ½ lemon

salt and freshly ground black pepper

boiled new potatoes and sliced carrots,
   to serve

1 Place the fish in a frying pan, add half the butter, the milk, fish stock, bay leaf and seasoning, and heat over medium heat to the simmering point. Lower the heat, cover the pan and poach the fish for 10–15 minutes, depending on the thickness of the fillets, until the fish is tender and the flesh just begins to flake.

2 Carefully transfer the fish to a warmed serving plate, cover and keep warm while you make the sauce. Return the cooking liquid to medium heat and bring to a boil, stirring. Simmer for about 4 minutes, then remove and discard the bay leaf.

3 Melt the remaining butter in a saucepan, stir in the flour and cook, stirring, for 1 minute. Remove from the heat and gradually stir in the fish cooking liquid. Return to the heat and bring to a boil, stirring constantly. Simmer for about 4 minutes, stirring frequently.

4 Remove the pan from the heat, blend the cream into the egg yolk, then stir into the sauce with the parsley. Reheat gently, stirring, for a few minutes.

5 Remove from the heat, add the lemon juice and rind and season to taste. Pour into a sauceboat. Serve the fish with the sauce, new potatoes and carrots.

Fish with Lemon, Red Onions and Cilantro

A rich mixture of flavors, textures and colors—and all produced in just one pan.

INGREDIENTS

Serves 4

4 halibut or cod steaks or cutlets, about 6 ounces each
juice of 1 lemon
1 teaspoon garlic powder
1 teaspoon paprika
1 teaspoon ground cumin
¾ teaspoon dried tarragon
¼ cup olive oil
flour, for dusting
1¼ cups fish stock
2 fresh red chilies, seeded and finely chopped
2 tablespoons chopped fresh cilantro
1 red onion, cut into rings
salt and freshly ground black pepper

1 Place the fish in a shallow non-metallic bowl and combine the lemon juice, garlic, paprika, cumin, tarragon and a little salt and pepper. Spoon the lemon mixture over the fish, cover loosely with plastic wrap and let marinate for a few hours or overnight in the refrigerator.

2 Gently heat 3 tablespoons of the oil in a large non-stick frying pan. Dust the fish with flour, then fry for a few minutes on each side, until golden brown all over.

3 Pour the fish stock around the fish, cover and simmer for about 5 minutes, until the fish is thoroughly cooked through.

4 Add the chopped red chilies and 1 tablespoon of the cilantro to the pan. Simmer for another 5 minutes.

5 Transfer the fish and sauce to a serving plate and keep warm.

6 Meanwhile, heat the remaining olive oil and stir-fry the onion rings until speckled brown. Scatter them over the fish with the remaining chopped cilantro and serve immediately.

Crumb-coated Shrimp

Serve these crunchy breaded shrimp with a homemade or store-bought dipping sauce of your choice.

·INGREDIENTS·

Serves 4

1½ cups polenta

about 1–2 teaspoons cayenne pepper

½ teaspoon ground cumin

1 teaspoon salt

2 tablespoons chopped fresh cilantro
    or parsley

2¼ pounds large raw shrimp, peeled
    and deveined

flour, for dredging

¼ cup vegetable oil

4 ounces coarsely grated Cheddar cheese

lime wedges and tomato salsa or relish,
    to serve

1 Mix the polenta, cayenne pepper, cumin, salt and cilantro in a bowl.

2 Coat the shrimp lightly in flour, then dip them in water and roll in the polenta mixture to coat evenly.

3 Heat the oil in a frying pan. When hot, add the shrimp, in batches if necessary. Cook for 2–3 minutes on each side, until they are cooked through. Drain on paper towels.

4 Preheat the broiler. Place the shrimp in a baking dish or in 4 individual flameproof dishes. Sprinkle on the cheese. Bake for 2–3 minutes. Serve with lime wedges and tomato salsa or relish.

Sweet-and-sour Shrimp

It is best to use raw shrimp if available. If you are using cooked ones, add them to the sauce without the initial deep-frying.

INGREDIENTS

Serves 4–6

1 pound raw jumbo shrimp in
   their shells
vegetable oil, for deep-frying
lettuce leaves, to serve

For the sauce

1 tablespoon vegetable oil
1 tablespoon finely chopped scallions
2 teaspoons finely chopped fresh
   ginger
2 tablespoons light soy sauce
2 tablespoons light brown sugar
3 tablespoons rice vinegar
1 tablespoon Chinese rice wine or
   dry sherry
about ½ cup chicken or vegetable stock
1 tablespoon cornstarch paste
few drops sesame oil

1 Pull the soft legs off the shrimp without removing the shells. Rinse and dry well with paper towels.

2 Heat the vegetable oil in a large pan or deep-fryer to 350°F and deep-fry the shrimp for 35–40 seconds or until their color changes from gray to bright orange. Remove and drain on paper towels.

3 To make the sauce, heat the oil in a preheated wok, add the scallions and ginger, followed by the seasonings and stock, and bring to a boil.

4 Add the shrimp to the sauce, blend well, then thicken the sauce with the cornstarch paste, stirring until smooth. Sprinkle with the sesame oil. Serve on a bed of lettuce.

Shrimp and Fish in an Herb Sauce

Bengalis are famous for their seafood dishes and always use mustard oil in recipes because it imparts a unique flavor and aroma. No feast is complete without one of these celebrated fish dishes.

INGREDIENTS

Serves 4–6

3 garlic cloves

2-inch piece fresh ginger

1 large leek, roughly chopped

4 green chilies

1 teaspoon vegetable oil (optional)

¼ cup mustard oil

1 tablespoon ground coriander

½ teaspoon fennel seeds

1 tablespoon crushed yellow mustard
     seeds or 1 teaspoon mustard powder

¾ cup thick coconut milk

8 ounces monkfish, sliced

8 ounces raw jumbo shrimp, peeled and
     deveined with tails intact

salt

1 bunch fresh cilantro leaves, chopped

green chilies, to garnish

3 Add the ground coriander, fennel seeds, mustard and coconut milk. Gently bring to a boil, then simmer, uncovered, for about 5 minutes.

4 Add the fish and simmer for 2 minutes, then fold in the shrimp and cook until the shrimp turn a bright orange-pink color. Season with salt, fold in the cilantro leaves and serve hot. Garnish with green chilies.

1 In a food processor, grind the garlic, ginger, leek and chilies into a coarse paste. Add vegetable oil if the mixture is too dry.

2 In a frying pan, heat the mustard oil with the paste until it is well blended. Keep the window open and take care not to overheat the mixture, as any smoke from the mustard oil will sting the eyes and irritate the nose.

Fish and Shrimp with Spinach and Coconut

The shrimp, spinach and coconut sauce provides a truly delightful medley of flavors to complement the fish.

INGREDIENTS

Serves 4

1 pound white fish fillets, such as cod
   or haddock
1 tablespoon lemon or lime juice
½ teaspoon garlic powder
1 teaspoon ground cinnamon
½ teaspoon dried thyme
½ teaspoon paprika
seasoned flour, for dusting
vegetable oil, for shallow frying
salt and freshly ground black pepper

For the sauce

2 tablespoons butter or margarine
1 onion, finely chopped
1 garlic clove, crushed
1¼ cups coconut milk
1 small bunch fresh spinach,
   finely sliced
8–10 ounces cooked peeled shrimp
1 fresh red chili, seeded and
   finely chopped

1 Place the fish fillets in a shallow bowl and sprinkle with the lemon or lime juice.

2 Combine the garlic powder, cinnamon, thyme, paprika and salt and pepper to taste. Sprinkle the seasoning over the fish, cover loosely with plastic wrap and let marinate in a cool place or in the refrigerator for a few hours.

3 Meanwhile, make the sauce. Melt the butter in a large heavy saucepan and fry the onion and garlic for 5–6 minutes, stirring frequently, until the onion is soft.

4 Place the coconut milk and spinach in a separate saucepan and bring to a boil. Cook gently for a few minutes until the spinach has wilted and the coconut milk has reduced a little, then set aside to cool slightly.

5 Blend the spinach mixture in a blender or food processor for 30 seconds and add to the onion, together with the shrimp and red chili. Stir well and simmer gently for a few minutes, then set aside while you cook the fish.

6 Cut the fish into 2-inch pieces and dip in the seasoned flour. Heat a little oil in a large frying pan and fry the fish pieces, in batches if necessary, for 2–3 minutes on each side, until golden brown. Drain thoroughly on paper towels.

7 Arrange the fish on a warmed serving plate. Gently reheat the sauce and serve separately in a sauceboat or poured over the fish.

Braised Fish in Chili and Garlic Sauce

This recipe reflects its Chinese origins. When served in a restaurant, the fish's head and tail are usually discarded before cooking and used in other dishes. A whole fish may be used, however, and always looks impressive, especially for formal occasions and dinner parties.

INGREDIENTS

Serves 4–6

1 carp, bream, sea bass, trout, grouper or
   striped mullet, weighing about
   1½ pounds, gutted
1 tablespoon light soy sauce
1 tablespoon Chinese rice wine or
   dry sherry
vegetable oil, for deep-frying

For the sauce
2 garlic cloves, finely chopped
2–3 scallions, finely chopped, with the
   white and green parts separated
1 teaspoon finely chopped fresh ginger
2 tablespoons hot bean sauce
1 tablespoon tomato paste
2 teaspoons light brown sugar
1 tablespoon rice vinegar
about ½ cup stock
1 tablespoon cornstarch paste
few drops sesame oil

1 Rinse and dry the fish. Score both sides of the fish, as deep as the bone, with diagonal cuts about 1 inch apart. Rub the fish with soy sauce and rice wine or sherry on both sides, then let marinate for 10–15 minutes.

2 Heat the oil in a preheated wok and deep-fry the fish for 3–4 minutes on both sides or until golden brown. Pour off the excess oil, leaving about 1 tablespoon in the wok.

3 Push the fish to one side of the wok and add the garlic, the white part of the scallions, chopped ginger, hot bean sauce, tomato paste, sugar, rice vinegar and stock. Bring to a boil and braise the fish in the sauce for 4–5 minutes, turning it over once. Add the green part of the scallions. Thicken the sauce with the cornstarch paste, sprinkle with the sesame oil, and serve immediately.

Tilapia in Fruit Sauce

Tilapia is widely used in African cooking, but can be found in most fishmongers. Yam or boiled yellow plantains are authentic—and very tasty—side dishes.

INGREDIENTS

Serves 4

4 tilapia, gutted and cleaned

½ lemon

2 garlic cloves, crushed

½ teaspoon dried thyme

2 tablespoons chopped scallions

vegetable oil, for shallow frying

flour, for dusting

2 tablespoons peanut oil

1 tablespoon butter or margarine

1 onion, finely chopped

3 tomatoes, skinned and finely chopped

1 teaspoon ground turmeric

¼ cup white wine

1 fresh green chili, seeded and
     finely chopped

2½ cups fish stock

1 teaspoon sugar

1 medium under-ripe mango, peeled,
     pitted and diced

1 tablespoon chopped fresh parsley

salt and freshly ground black pepper

1 Place the fish in a shallow bowl, squeeze lemon juice all over it and gently rub in the garlic, thyme and some salt and pepper. Place some of the scallion in the cavity of each fish, cover loosely with plastic wrap and let marinate for a few hours or overnight in the refrigerator.

2 Heat a little vegetable oil in a large frying pan, coat the fish with flour, then fry the fish on both sides for a few minutes, until golden brown. Remove from the pan to a plate, using a slotted spoon, and set aside.

3 Heat the peanut oil and butter in a saucepan and fry the onion for 4–5 minutes, until soft. Stir in the tomatoes and cook briskly for a few minutes.

4 Add the turmeric, white wine, chili, fish stock and sugar, stir well and bring to a boil, then cover and simmer gently for 10 minutes.

5 Add the fish and cook over low heat for 15–20 minutes, until the fish is cooked through. Add the mango, arranging it around the fish, and cook briefly for 1–2 minutes to heat through.

6 Arrange the fish on a warmed serving plate with the mango and tomato sauce poured on top. Garnish with chopped parsley and serve immediately.

Spanish-style Hake

Cod and haddock cutlets will also work well in this recipe.

Serves 4

2 tablespoons olive oil

2 tablespoons butter

1 onion, chopped

3 garlic cloves, crushed

1 tablespoon flour

½ teaspoon paprika

4 hake cutlets, about 6 ounces each

8 ounces fine green beans, cut into
  1-inch lengths

1½ cups fresh fish stock

⅔ cup dry white wine

2 tablespoons dry sherry

16–20 fresh mussels, cleaned

3 tablespoons chopped fresh parsley

salt and freshly ground black pepper

crusty bread, to serve

1 Heat the oil and butter in a sauté or frying pan, add the onion and cook for 5 minutes, until softened, but not browned. Add the crushed garlic and cook for 1 more minute.

2 Combine the plain flour and paprika, then lightly dust over the hake cutlets. Push the onion and garlic to one side of the frying pan. Add the hake cutlets to the frying pan and fry until golden on both sides.

3 Stir in the beans, stock, wine, sherry and seasoning. Bring to a boil and cook for 2 minutes.

4 Add the mussels and parsley, cover and cook for 5–8 minutes, until all the mussels open. Discard any closed ones.

5 Serve in warmed shallow bowls, with crusty bread.

Halibut with Tomato Vinaigrette

Sauce vierge, an uncooked mixture of tomatoes, aromatic fresh herbs and olive oil, can either be served at room temperature or, as in this dish, tiède (slightly warm).

INGREDIENTS

Serves 4

3 large ripe beefsteak tomatoes, skinned, seeded and chopped

2 shallots or 1 small red onion, finely chopped

1 garlic clove, crushed

6 tablespoons chopped mixed fresh herbs, such as parsley, cilantro, basil, tarragon, chervil or chives

½ cup extra virgin olive oil

4 halibut fillets or steaks, 6–7 ounces each

salt and freshly ground black pepper

green salad, to serve

1 In a medium bowl, combine the tomatoes, shallots or onion, garlic and herbs. Stir in the oil and season with salt and freshly ground black pepper. Cover the bowl and set aside at room temperature for about 1 hour to let the flavors blend.

2 Preheat the broiler. Line a broiler pan with foil and brush the foil lightly with oil.

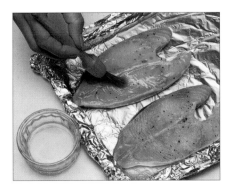

3 Season the fish with salt and pepper. Place the fish on the foil and brush with a little extra oil. Broil for 5–6 minutes, until the fish is lightly browned and cooked through.

4 Pour the sauce into a saucepan and heat gently for a few minutes. Serve the fish with the sauce and a green salad.

Seafood Balti with Vegetables

In this dish, the spicy seafood is cooked separately and combined with the vegetables at the last minute to create a truly delicious combination of flavors.

INGREDIENTS

Serves 4

8 ounces cod

8 ounces cooked peeled shrimp

6 crab sticks, halved lengthwise

1 tablespoon lemon juice

1 teaspoon ground coriander

1 teaspoon chili powder

1 teaspoon salt

1 teaspoon ground cumin

¼ cup cornstarch

⅔ cup corn oil

For the vegetables

⅔ cup corn oil

2 medium onions, chopped

1 teaspoon onion seeds

½ medium cauliflower, cut into florets

4 ounces green beans, cut into
   1-inch lengths

½ cup corn

1 teaspoon shredded fresh ginger

1 teaspoon chili powder

1 teaspoon salt

4 fresh green chilies, sliced

2 tablespoons chopped fresh cilantro

lime slices, to garnish

1 Skin the fish and cut into small cubes. Put into a medium-size mixing bowl, add the shrimp and crab sticks and set aside.

2 In a separate bowl, combine the lemon juice, ground coriander, chili powder, salt and ground cumin. Pour this over the seafood and combine thoroughly, using your hands.

3 Sprinkle on the cornstarch and mix again until the seafood is well coated. Set to one side in the refrigerator for about 1 hour to let the flavors develop.

4 To make the vegetable mixture, heat the oil in a preheated wok. Add the onions and onion seeds and stir-fry until lightly browned.

5 Add the cauliflower, green beans, corn, ginger, chili powder, salt, green chilies and fresh cilantro. Stir-fry for 7–10 minutes over medium heat.

6 Spoon the fried vegetables around the edge of a shallow dish, leaving a space in the middle for the seafood, and keep warm.

7 Wash and dry the wok or karahi, then heat the oil to fry the seafood pieces. Fry the seafood pieces in 2–3 batches, until they turn a golden brown. Remove with a slotted spoon and drain well on paper towels.

8 Arrange the batches of seafood in the middle of the dish of vegetables and keep warm while you fry the remaining seafood. Garnish with lime slices and serve.

Chunky Fish Balti with Bell Peppers

Try to find as many differently colored sweet peppers as possible to make this very attractive dish.

INGREDIENTS

Serves 2–4

1 pound cod, or any other firm white fish

1½ teaspoons ground cumin

2 teaspoons mango powder

1 teaspoon ground coriander

½ teaspoon chili powder

1 teaspoon ginger pulp

3 tablespoons cornstarch

⅔ cup corn oil

3 colored bell peppers, seeded and chopped

salt

8–10 cherry tomatoes, to garnish

1 Skin the fish and cut it into small cubes. Put the fish cubes into a large mixing bowl and add the ground cumin, mango powder, ground coriander, chili powder, 1 teaspoon salt, ginger pulp and cornstarch. Combine thoroughly, using 2 spoons or your hands, until the fish is well coated.

2 Heat the oil in a preheated wok or karahi. Lower the heat and add the fish pieces, 3 or 4 at a time. Fry for about 3 minutes, turning and moving them constantly.

3 Drain the fish on paper towels. Transfer to a serving dish and keep warm while you fry the remaining fish pieces.

4 Add the peppers to the wok or karahi and fry for 2 minutes. They should still be slightly crisp. Drain on paper towels.

5 Add the drained peppers to the serving dish and garnish with the cherry tomatoes. Serve immediately.

Chinese-spiced Fish Fillets

East meets West with this novel twist on a classic English dish.

INGREDIENTS

Serves 4

¾ cup flour

1 teaspoon Chinese five-spice powder

8 skinned fillets of fish, such as plaice or lemon sole, about 1¾ pounds total

1 egg, beaten to mix

½ cup fine fresh bread crumbs

peanut oil, for frying

2 tablespoons butter

4 scallions, cut diagonally into thin slices

2 large tomatoes, seeded and diced

2 tablespoons soy sauce

salt and freshly ground black pepper

chives and strips of red bell pepper, to garnish

1 Sift the flour together with the Chinese five-spice powder and salt and pepper to taste onto a plate. Dip the fish fillets first in the seasoned flour, then in beaten egg and finally in bread crumbs.

2 Pour the oil into a large frying pan to a depth of ½ inch. Heat until it is very hot and starting to sizzle. Add the coated fillets, a few at a time, and fry for 2–3 minutes, according to the thickness of the fillets, until just cooked and golden brown on both sides. Do not crowd the pan or the temperature of the oil will drop and the fish will absorb too much oil.

3 Drain the fillets on paper towels, then transfer to plates and keep warm. Pour off all the oil from the frying pan and wipe it out with paper towels.

4 Melt the butter in the pan and add the scallions and tomatoes. Stir-fry for 1 minute. Stir in the soy sauce.

5 Spoon the tomato mixture over the fish and serve immediately, garnished with the chives and pepper strips.

Salmon with Watercress Sauce

Adding the watercress right at the end of cooking lets it retain much of its flavor and color.

Serves 4

1¼ cups crème fraîche

2 tablespoons chopped fresh tarragon

2 tablespoons unsalted butter

1 tablespoon sunflower oil

4 salmon fillets, skinned and boned

1 garlic clove, crushed

scant ½ cup dry white wine

1 bunch watercress

salt and freshly ground black pepper

salad greens, to serve

1 Gently heat the crème fraîche in a small pan until just beginning to boil. Remove the pan from the heat and stir in half the tarragon. Let the herb cream infuse while you cook the fish.

2 Heat the butter and oil in a frying pan, add the salmon and fry for 3–5 minutes on each side. Remove from the pan and keep warm.

3 Add the garlic to the pan and fry for 1 minute, then pour in the wine and let it bubble until reduced to about 1 tablespoon.

4 Meanwhile, strip the leaves off the watercress stalks and chop finely. Discard any damaged leaves. (Save the watercress stalks for soup, if desired.)

5 Strain the herb cream into the pan and cook for a few minutes, stirring until the sauce has thickened. Stir in the remaining chopped tarragon and the watercress, then cook for a few minutes, until wilted but still bright green. Season and serve immediately, spooned over the salmon. Serve with salad greens.

Salmon with Green Peppercorns

A fashionable discovery of nouvelle cuisine, green peppercorns add piquancy to all kinds of sauces and stews. Available pickled in jars or cans, they are great to keep on hand in your pantry.

INGREDIENTS

Serves 4

1 tablespoon butter

2 or 3 shallots, finely chopped

1 tablespoon brandy (optional)

¼ cup white wine

6 tablespoons fish or chicken stock

½ cup heavy cream

2–3 tablespoons green peppercorns in brine, rinsed

1–2 tablespoons vegetable oil

4 pieces salmon fillct, 6–7 ounces each

salt and freshly ground black pepper

fresh parsley, to garnish

1 Melt the butter in a heavy saucepan over medium heat. Add the shallots and cook for 1–2 minutes, until just softened but not colored.

2 Add the brandy, if using, and the white wine, then add the stock and bring to a boil. Boil vigorously to reduce by three-quarters, stirring occasionally.

3 Reduce the heat, then add the cream and half the pepper-corns, crushing them slightly with the back of a spoon. Cook very gently for 4–5 minutes, until the sauce is slightly thickened, then strain and stir in the remaining peppercorns. Keep the sauce warm over very low heat, stirring occasionally, while you cook the salmon fillets.

4 In a large heavy frying pan, heat the oil over medium-high heat until very hot. Lightly season the salmon and cook for 3–4 minutes, until the flesh is opaque throughout. To check, pierce the fish with the tip of a sharp knife; the juices should run clear. Arrange the fish on warmed plates and pour on the sauce. Garnish with parsley and serve.

Salmon with Tarragon Mushroom Sauce

Tarragon has a distinctive aniseed flavor that is good with fish, cream and mushrooms. This recipe uses oyster mushrooms to provide both texture and flavor.

INGREDIENTS

Serves 4

4 tablespoons (½ stick) unsalted butter

4 salmon steaks, 6 ounces each

1 shallot, finely chopped

6 ounces assorted wild and cultivated
   mushrooms, such as oyster
   mushrooms, trimmed and sliced

scant 1 cup chicken or vegetable stock

2 teaspoons cornstarch

½ teaspoon mustard

¼ cup crème fraîche

3 tablespoons chopped fresh tarragon

1 teaspoon white wine vinegar

salt and cayenne pepper

boiled new potatoes and green salad,
   to serve

1 Melt half the butter in a large frying pan, season the salmon and cook over medium heat for 8 minutes, turning once. Transfer to a plate, cover and keep warm.

2 Heat the remaining butter in the pan and gently fry the shallot to soften. Add the mushrooms and cook until the juices begin to flow. Add the stock and simmer for 2–3 minutes.

3 Combine the cornstarch and mustard and blend with 1 tablespoon of water. Stir into the mushroom mixture and bring to a simmer, stirring, to thicken. Add the crème fraîche, tarragon, vinegar and salt and pepper to taste.

4 Spoon the mushrooms and sauce over each salmon steak and serve with new potatoes and a green salad.

COOK'S TIP

Fresh tarragon will bruise and darken quickly after chopping, so prepare the herb just before you need it.

Grilled Butterflied Salmon

*Ask your fishmonger to bone the
salmon for butterflying.*

INGREDIENTS

Serves 6–8

1½ tablespoons dried juniper berries

2 teaspoons dried green peppercorns

1 teaspoon superfine sugar

3 tablespoons vegetable oil

2 tablespoons lemon juice

5–5¼ pounds salmon, scaled, gutted and
   boned for butterflying

salt

lemon wedges and parsley sprigs,
   to garnish

1 Grind the juniper berries and
peppercorns in a spice mill or
in a mortar with a pestle. Transfer
the ground spices to a small bowl
and stir in the sugar, oil, lemon
juice and salt to taste.

2 Open the salmon like a book,
skin side down. Spread the
juniper mixture evenly over the
flesh. Fold the salmon closed again
and place on a large plate. Cover
and marinate in the refrigerator
for at least 1 hour.

3 Open up the salmon again and
place it, skin side down, on an
oiled baking sheet. Spoon any
juniper mixture left on the plate
over the fish.

4 Cook under a preheated
broiler, about 4 inches from
the heat, for 8–10 minutes or until
the fish is cooked. Serve the fish
immediately, garnished with the
lemon wedges and parsley.

COOK'S TIP

To bone the salmon yourself,
follow the instructions for boning
a round fish through the stomach.
Remove both the head and tail
but do not separate the fillets.

Mackerel California Style

Fish, coated with spices, are often fried until "blackened" in California, but this does make a lot of smoke in the kitchen. This recipe doesn't go quite that far.

INGREDIENTS

Serves 2–4

2 teaspoon paprika

1½ teaspoons salt

½ teaspoon onion powder

½ teaspoon garlic powder

½ teaspoon white pepper

½ teaspoon black pepper

½ teaspoon dried dill

½ teaspoon dried oregano

2 large thick mackerel, boned and filleted

8 tablespoons (1 stick) butter

lemon slices and oregano sprigs,
   to garnish

1 Combine the seasonings. Dip each fillet of mackerel into the spice mixture until well coated.

2 Heat half the butter in a large frying pan until really hot. Add the fish and cook, 2 fillets at a time, for about 2 minutes on each side. Remove immediately, add the rest of the butter and then cook the remaining fillets.

3 Serve piping hot with a little of the butter from the pan poured on top and garnished with lemon slices and sprigs of oregano.

COOK'S TIP
∾

Other fish, such as salmon, red snapper and tuna, are also suitable, but thick cuts are best.

Trout with Curried Orange Butter

Small trout are perfect midweek fare and delicious served with this tangy butter. Children particularly like the buttery curry flavor, but it is a good idea to fillet the cooked trout and remove the bones before serving this to very young children.

INGREDIENTS

Serves 4

2 tablespoons butter, softened

1 teaspoon curry powder

1 teaspoon grated orange rind

4 small trout, gutted and heads removed

a little oil

salt and freshly ground black pepper

4 wedges of orange, to garnish

boiled new potatoes, to serve

1 Combine the butter, curry powder, orange rind and seasoning, wrap in foil and freeze for 10 minutes.

2 Brush the fish all over with oil and sprinkle well with seasoning. Make three diagonal slashes through the skin and flesh, on each side of the fish.

3 Cut the flavored butter into small pieces and insert into the slashes. Place the fish on the broiler pan and cook under a preheated broiler for 3–4 minutes on each side, depending on the thickness. Serve the fish, garnished with wedges of orange, with boiled new potatoes.

Cod, Basil and Tomato with a Potato Crust

With a green salad, this makes an ideal dish for a substantial lunch or a family supper.

INGREDIENTS

Serves 8

2¼ pounds cod fillet

2¼ pounds smoked cod fillet

2½ cups milk

5 cups water

2 basil sprigs

1 sprig lemon thyme

6 tablespoons (¾ stick) butter

1 onion, chopped

2 tablespoons flour

2 tablespoons tomato paste

2 tablespoons chopped basil

12 medium potatoes

4 tablespoons (½ stick) butter

1¼ cups milk

salt and freshly ground black pepper

1 tablespoon chopped parsley, to serve

1 Place the cod fillet and smoked cod fillet in a roasting pan with the milk, water, basil sprigs and sprig of lemon thyme. Simmer over low heat for 3–4 minutes. Let cool in the cooking liquid for about 20 minutes. Drain the fish, reserving the liquid for use in the sauce. Flake the fish, taking care to remove any skin and bones.

2 Melt the butter in a pan, add the onion and cook for about 5 minutes, until tender but not browned. Add the flour, tomato paste and half the chopped basil. Gradually add the reserved fish cooking liquid, adding a little more milk, if necessary, to make a fairly thin sauce. Bring to the boil, season to taste with salt and pepper, and add the remaining chopped basil. Add the fish carefully and stir gently. Transfer the mixture to an ovenproof dish.

3 Boil the potatoes until tender. Add the butter and milk and mash well. Add salt and pepper to taste and spread over the fish mixture, forking to create a pattern. Bake in a preheated oven at 350°F for about 30 minutes, or until heated through. Serve with the chopped parsley.

Creamy Fish and Mushroom Pie

Fish pie is a healthy and hearty dish for a hungry family. Mushrooms go well with the fish and provide additional flavor and nourishment.

INGREDIENTS

Serves 4

8 ounces assorted wild and cultivated
 mushrooms, such as oyster, button or
 chanterelle, trimmed and quartered
1½ pounds cod or haddock fillet, skinned
 and diced
2½ cups milk, boiling

For the topping

2 pounds floury potatoes, quartered
2 tablespoons butter
⅔ cup milk
salt and freshly ground black pepper
grated nutmeg

For the sauce

4 tablespoons (½ stick) unsalted butter
1 medium onion, chopped
½ celery stalk, chopped
2 tablespoons flour
2 teaspoons lemon juice
3 tablespoons chopped fresh parsley

1 Grease an ovenproof dish, scatter the mushrooms over the base, add the fish and season with salt and pepper to taste. Pour in the boiling milk, cover the dish and cook at 400°F for 20 minutes.

2 Using a slotted spoon, transfer the fish and mushrooms to a 6-cup baking dish. Pour the poaching liquid into a bowl and reserve for use in the sauce.

3 Meanwhile, cook the potatoes in lightly salted boiling water for 20 minutes. Drain and mash with the butter and milk. Season well with salt, pepper and nutmeg.

4 To make the sauce, melt the butter in a saucepan, add the onion and celery and fry until soft, but not colored. Stir in the flour, then remove from the heat.

5 Gradually add the reserved liquid, stirring until absorbed. Return to the heat, stir and simmer to thicken. Add the lemon juice and parsley, season, then add to the baking dish.

6 Top with the mashed potatoes and return to the oven for 30–40 minutes, until the topping is golden brown.

Crunchy-topped Cod

Colorful and quick to cook, this is an ideal dish for weekday meals.

Serves 4

4 pieces cod fillet, about 4 ounces
    each, skinned
2 medium tomatoes, sliced
½ cup fresh whole wheat bread crumbs
2 tablespoons chopped fresh parsley
finely grated rind and juice of ½ lemon
1 teaspoon sunflower oil
salt and freshly ground black pepper
mixed fresh vegetables, to serve

1 Arrange the cod fillets in a wide ovenproof dish.

2 Arrange the tomato slices on top. Combine the bread crumbs, fresh parsley, lemon rind and juice and the oil with seasoning to taste.

3 Spoon the crumb mixture evenly over the fish, then bake at 400°F for 15–20 minutes. Serve hot with mixed fresh vegetables.

Special Fish Pie

This fish pie is colorful, healthy and—best of all—very easy to make. For a more economical version, omit the shrimp and replace with more haddock fillet.

Serves 4

12 ounces haddock fillet, skinned
2 tablespoons cornstarch
4 ounces cooked peeled shrimp
1 can (7 ounces) corn, drained
½ cup frozen peas
⅔ cup milk
4 ounces (½ package) cream cheese
¼ cup fresh whole wheat bread crumbs
1½ ounces grated Cheddar cheese
salt and freshly ground black pepper
mixed fresh vegetables, to serve

1 Cut the haddock into bite-size pieces and toss in cornstarch to coat evenly.

2 Place the fish, shrimp, corn and peas in an ovenproof dish. Beat together the milk, cream cheese and seasonings, then pour into the dish.

3 Combine the bread crumbs and grated cheese, then spoon evenly over the top of the dish. Bake in a preheated oven at 375°F for 25–30 minutes or until golden brown. Serve hot with mixed fresh vegetables.

Golden Fish Pie

Crispy, crunchy filo pastry makes a wonderful contrast to the creamy fish filling.

INGREDIENTS

Serves 4–6

1½ pounds white fish fillets

1¼ cups milk

2 slices onion

2 bay leaves

6 black peppercorns

4 ounces cooked peeled shrimp, defrosted if frozen

8 tablespoons (1 stick) butter

2 tablespoons flour

1¼ cups light cream or half-and-half

3 ounces Gruyère cheese, grated

1 bunch watercress, leaves only, chopped

1 teaspoon Dijon mustard

5 sheets filo pastry

salt and freshly ground black pepper

3 Melt 4 tablespoons (½ stick) of the butter in a pan. Stir in the flour and cook for 1 minute. Stir in the reserved cooking liquid and the cream or half-and-half. Bring to a boil, stirring continuously, then simmer for 2–3 minutes, until the sauce has thickened.

4 Remove the pan from the heat and stir in the grated Gruyère, watercress, mustard and seasoning to taste. Pour over the fish and set aside to cool.

5 Melt the remaining butter. Brush 1 sheet of filo pastry with a little melted butter, then crumple up loosely and place on top of the filling. Repeat with the remaining filo sheets and butter until they are all used up and the pie is completely covered.

6 Bake at 375°F for 25–30 minutes, or until heated through and the pastry is golden and crisp.

1 Place the fish fillets in a pan, pour in the milk and add the onion slices, bay leaves and peppercorns. Bring just to a boil, then cover and simmer for about 10–12 minutes, until the fish is almost tender.

2 Remove the fish from the pan with a slotted spoon. Skin and remove any bones, then roughly flake into a shallow ovenproof dish. Scatter the peeled shrimp over the fish. Strain the cooking liquid and reserve.

Cod with Lentils and Leeks

This unusual dish, discovered in a Parisian charcuterie, is great for entertaining. You can cook the vegetables ahead of time and let it bake while the first course is served.

INGREDIENTS

Serves 4

5 ounces green lentils

1 bay leaf

1 garlic clove, finely chopped

grated rind of 1 orange

grated rind of 1 lemon

pinch of ground cumin

1 tablespoon butter

1 pound leeks, thinly sliced or cut into
   julienne strips

1¼ cups whipping cream

1 tablespoon lemon juice, or to taste

1¾ pounds thick skinless cod or
   haddock fillets

salt and freshly ground black pepper

1 Rinse the lentils and put them in a saucepan with the bay leaf and garlic. Add enough water to cover by 2 inches. Bring to a boil and boil gently for 10 minutes, then reduce the heat and simmer for another 15–30 minutes, until the lentils are just tender.

2 Drain the lentils and discard the bay leaf, then stir in half the orange rind and all the lemon rind and season with ground cumin and salt and pepper. Transfer to a shallow baking dish or gratin dish.

3 Melt the butter in a saucepan over medium heat, then add the leeks and cook, stirring frequently, until just softened. Add 1 cup of the cream and the remaining orange rind and cook gently for 15–20 minutes. Stir in the lemon juice and season with salt and plenty of pepper.

4 Cut the fish into 4 pieces and pull out any small bones. Season the fish with salt and pepper, place on top of the lentil mixture and press down slightly into the lentils.

5 Cover each piece of fish with a quarter of the leek mixture and pour 1 tablespoon of the remaining cream over each. Bake at 375°F for about 30 minutes, until the fish is cooked through and the topping is lightly golden.

Salmon Coulibiac

This is a complicated Russian dish that takes a lot of preparation, but is well worth the work. Traditionally sturgeon is used but, as this is difficult to obtain, salmon may be substituted. As a special treat, serve with shots of chilled vodka for an authentic Russian flavor.

INGREDIENTS

Serves 8

butter, for greasing

flour, for dusting

1 pound puff pastry

1 egg, beaten

salt and freshly ground black pepper

lemon wedges and fresh dill sprigs,
    to garnish

For the pancakes

2 eggs, separated

3 cups milk

1 cup flour

3 sticks butter, melted

½ teaspoon salt

½ teaspoon superfine sugar

For the filling

4 tablespoons (½ stick) butter

12 ounces chestnut mushrooms, sliced

scant ½ cup white wine

juice of ½ lemon

1½ pounds salmon fillet, skinned

1 cup long grain rice

2 tablespoons chopped fresh dill

1 large onion, chopped

4 hard-cooked eggs, shelled and sliced

1 First, make the pancakes. Whisk the egg yolks together and add the milk. Gradually beat in the flour, the melted butter (reserving 1 tablespoon), salt and sugar until smooth. Let stand for about 30 minutes.

2 Whisk the egg whites until they just form stiff peaks, then fold into the batter. Heat a little of the remaining butter in a heavy frying pan and add about 3 tablespoons of the batter. Turn and cook until golden. Repeat until all the mixture has been used up, brushing on a little melted butter when stacking the pancakes. When they are cool, cut into long rectangles, cover and set aside.

3 For the filling, melt most of the butter in a heavy frying pan, add the mushrooms and cook for 3 minutes. Add ¼ cup of the wine and boil for 2 minutes, then simmer for about 5 more minutes. Add almost all the remaining wine and the lemon juice.

4 Place the salmon on top of the cooked mushrooms, cover with foil, and gently steam for 8–10 minutes, until just cooked. Remove the salmon from the pan and set aside.

5 Set aside the mushrooms and pour the cooking liquid into a large clean pan. Add the rice and cook for 10–15 minutes, until tender, adding more wine if necessary. Remove from the heat and stir in the dill and seasoning. Melt the remaining butter and fry the onion until brown. Set aside.

6 Grease a large baking sheet. Flour a clean dish towel, place the pastry on it and roll into a 12 x 20-inch rectangle. Leaving 1¼ inches at the top and bottom ends of the pastry, place half the pancakes in a strip up the middle of the dough. Top with half the rice, half the onion, half the eggs and half the mushrooms. Place the salmon on top of the mushrooms and press down gently. Continue the layering process in reverse.

7 Take the 1¼-inch ends and wrap over the filling, then fold over the long edges. Brush with beaten egg and transfer to the baking sheet, rolling it so that it ends up seam side down. Chill for 1 hour. Cut 4 small slits in the top, brush with beaten egg and bake at 425°F for 10 minutes. Turn the oven down to 375°F and cook for another 30 minutes, until golden brown. Serve sliced, garnished with lemon and dill.

Creamy Creole Crab

Serves 6

2 cans (7 ounces each) crab meat

3 hard-cooked eggs, shelled

1 teaspoon Dijon mustard

6 tablespoons (¾ stick) butter or
    margarine

¼ teaspoon cayenne pepper

3 tablespoons sherry

2 tablespoons chopped fresh parsley

½ cup light cream or half-and-half

2–3 thinly sliced scallions, including some
    of the green parts

¼ cup dried white bread crumbs

salt and freshly ground black pepper

fresh chives and flat leaf parsley sprigs,
    to garnish

1 Flake the crab meat into a medium-size bowl, keeping the pieces of crab as large as possible and removing any stray pieces of shell or cartilage.

2 In another bowl, crumble the egg yolks with a fork. Add the mustard, 4 tablespoons of the butter and the cayenne pepper, then mash together to form a paste. Mix in the sherry and parsley.

3 Chop the egg whites and mix in with the cream or half-and-half and scallions. Stir in the crab meat and season well.

4 Divide the crab mixture equally among 6 greased scallop shells or individual baking dishes. Sprinkle with the bread crumbs and dot with the remaining butter.

5 Bake at 350°F for about 20 minutes, until bubbling hot and golden brown. Serve, garnished with fresh chives and flat leaf parsley sprigs.

Crab with Scallions and Ginger

This recipe is far less complicated to make than it first appears. Buy live crabs, if you can, for the best flavor and texture.

INGREDIENTS

Serves 4

1 large or 2 medium crabs, cooked, weighing about 1½ pounds in total

2 tablespoons Chinese rice wine or dry sherry

1 egg, lightly beaten

1 tablespoon cornstarch paste

3–4 tablespoons vegetable oil

1 tablespoon finely chopped fresh ginger

3–4 scallions, cut into short sections

2 tablespoons light soy sauce

1 teaspoon light brown sugar

about 5 tablespoons vegetable or chicken stock

few drops sesame oil

shredded scallion, to garnish

stir-fried noodles, to serve

3 Heat the oil in a preheated wok and stir-fry the crab pieces, together with the chopped ginger and scallions, for 2–3 minutes.

4 Add the soy sauce, sugar and stock and blend well. Bring to a boil, cover and braise for 3–4 minutes. Sprinkle with sesame oil, garnish with scallions and serve with stir-fried noodles.

1 Cut the crab in half from the underbelly. Break off the claws and crack them with the back of a cleaver. Discard the legs and crack the shell, breaking it into several pieces. Discard the feathery gills and the sac.

2 Put the crab pieces in a bowl. Combine the rice wine or sherry, egg and cornstarch paste, pour over the crab and set aside to marinate for 10–15 minutes.

Shrimp Soufflé

This makes a very elegant lunch dish and is simple to prepare.

Serves 4–6

2 tablespoons butter, plus extra for greasing

1 tablespoon dried white bread crumbs

6 ounces cooked peeled shrimp, deveined and coarsely chopped

1 tablespoon finely chopped fresh tarragon or parsley

3 tablespoons sherry or dry white wine

freshly ground black pepper

lemon slices, whole shrimp and flat leaf parsley sprig, to garnish

For the soufflé mixture

3 tablespoons butter

2½ tablespoons flour

1 cup milk, heated

4 eggs, separated, plus 1 egg white

salt

1 Butter a 7-cup soufflé dish. Sprinkle with the bread crumbs, tilting the dish to coat the bottom and sides evenly.

2 Melt the butter in a small saucepan. Add the chopped shrimp and cook for 2–3 minutes over low heat. Stir in the tarragon or parsley and sherry and season with pepper. Cook for another 1–2 minutes. Raise the heat and boil rapidly to evaporate the liquid, then remove from the heat and set aside.

3 To make the soufflé mixture, melt the butter in a heavy saucepan. Add the flour, blending well with a wire whisk. Cook over low heat for 2–3 minutes. Pour in the hot milk and whisk vigorously until smooth. Simmer for 2 minutes, still whisking, then season to taste with salt.

4 Remove the pan from the heat and immediately beat in the egg yolks, 1 at a time. Stir in the shrimp mixture.

5 Whisk the egg whites in a large bowl until they form stiff peaks. Stir about one-quarter of the egg whites into the shrimp mixture, then gently fold in the rest of the egg whites.

6 Carefully turn the mixture into the prepared dish. Bake at 375°F for 30–40 minutes, until the soufflé is puffed up and light golden brown on top. Serve immediately, with lemon slices, whole shrimp and a parsley sprig garnish.

VARIATIONS

For lobster soufflé, substitute 1 large lobster tail for the cooked shrimp. Chop it finely and add to the saucepan with the herbs and wine in place of the shrimp. For crab soufflé, instead of shrimp, use about 6-ounces fresh crab meat or a 7-ounce can, drained. Flake and pick over carefully to remove any bits of shell.

Baked Mussels and Potatoes

This dish originates from Púglia in southern Italy, a region noted for its imaginative baked dishes.

INGREDIENTS

Serves 2–3

1½ pounds large mussels, in their shells

1 cup water

8 ounces potatoes, unpeeled

5 tablespoons olive oil

2 garlic cloves, finely chopped

8 fresh basil leaves, torn into pieces

2 large tomatoes, skinned and
 thinly sliced

3 tablespoons bread crumbs

salt and freshly ground black pepper

1 Cut off the "beards" from the mussels. Scrub and soak in several changes of cold water. Discard any with broken shells and ones that do not shut immediately when tapped sharply. Place the mussels with the water in a large saucepan over medium heat. As soon as they open, lift them out. Remove and discard the empty half shells, leaving the mussels in the other half. (Discard any mussels that do not open.) Strain any liquid in the pan through a layer of paper towels and reserve.

2 Cook the potatoes in lightly salted boiling water until they are cooked, but still quite firm. Drain, peel and slice them.

3 Pour 2 tablespoons of the olive oil into the base of a shallow ovenproof dish and tilt to coat. Cover with the potato slices in a single layer. Add the mussels in their half shells in a single layer. Sprinkle with chopped garlic and pieces of basil.

4 Cover with a layer of the tomato slices. Sprinkle with the bread crumbs and black pepper, the reserved mussel cooking liquid and the remaining olive oil. Bake at 350°F for about 20 minutes or until the tomatoes are soft and the bread crumbs golden. Serve immediately.

Seafood in Puff Pastry

This classic combination of seafood in a creamy sauce served in a puff pastry case is found as an hors d'oeuvre on the menus of many elegant restaurants in France.

INGREDIENTS

Serves 6

butter, for greasing

12 ounces puff pastry

1 egg beaten with 1 tablespoon water, to glaze

¼ cup dry white wine

2 shallots, finely chopped

1 pound mussels, scrubbed and "debearded"

1 tablespoon butter

1 pound shelled scallops, cut in half horizontally

1 pound raw shrimp, peeled and deveined

6 ounces cooked lobster meat, sliced

For the sauce

2 sticks unsalted butter, diced

2 shallots, finely chopped

1 cup fish stock

6 tablespoons dry white wine

1–2 tablespoons heavy cream

lemon juice

salt and freshly ground white pepper

fresh dill sprigs, to garnish

1 Lightly grease a large baking sheet and sprinkle with a little water. On a lightly floured surface, roll out the pastry into a rectangle slightly less than ¼ inch thick. Using a sharp knife, cut into 6 diamond shapes about 5 inches long. Transfer to the baking sheet. Brush the pastry with the egg glaze. Using the tip of a knife, score a line ½ inch from the edge, then lightly mark the center in a crisscross pattern.

2 Chill the pastry shells for 30 minutes. Bake at 425°F for about 20 minutes, until puffed and golden brown. Transfer to a wire rack and, while still hot, remove each lid, cutting along the scored line to free it. Scoop out any uncooked dough from the bases and discard, then set the shells aside and let them cool completely.

3 In a large saucepan, bring the wine and shallots to a boil over high heat. Add the mussels to the pan, cover tightly and cook, shaking the pan occasionally, for 4–6 minutes, until the shells open. Remove and discard any mussels that do not open. Reserve 6 mussels for the garnish, then remove the rest of the mussels from their shells and set aside in a bowl, covered. Strain the cooking liquid through a muslin-lined sieve and reserve for the sauce.

4 In a heavy frying pan, melt the butter over medium heat. Add the scallops and shrimp, cover tightly and cook for 3–4 minutes, shaking and stirring occasionally, until they feel just firm to the touch; do not overcook.

5 Using a slotted spoon, transfer the scallops and shrimp to the bowl with the mussels and add any cooking juices to the reserved mussel cooking liquid.

6 To make the sauce, melt 2 tablespoons of the butter in a heavy saucepan. Add the shallots and cook for 2 minutes. Pour in the fish stock and boil for about 15 minutes over high heat, until reduced by three-quarters. Add the white wine and reserved cooking liquid and boil for 5–7 minutes, until reduced by half. Lower the heat to medium and whisk in the remaining butter, a little at a time, to make a smooth thick sauce (lift the pan from the heat if the sauce begins to boil). Whisk in the cream and season with salt, if needed, pepper and lemon juice. Keep the sauce warm over very low heat, stirring frequently.

7 Warm the pastry shells in a low oven for about 10 minutes. Put the mussels, scallops and shrimp in a large saucepan. Stir in a quarter of the sauce and reheat gently over low heat. Gently stir in the lobster meat and cook for 1 more minute.

8 Arrange the pastry shell bases on individual plates. Divide the seafood mixture equally among them and top with the lids. Garnish each with a mussel in its half shell and a dill sprig and spoon the remaining sauce around the edges or serve separately.

Puff Pastry Salmon with Chanterelle Cream

The slightly bland flavor of farmed salmon is helped by a creamy layer of chanterelle mushrooms.

INGREDIENTS

Serves 6

1½ pounds puff pastry, thawed
    if frozen

1 egg, beaten, to glaze

2 large salmon fillets, about 2 pounds
    total weight, skinned and boned

1½ cups dry white wine

1 small carrot

1 small onion, halved

½ celery stalk, chopped

1 thyme sprig

kale, to garnish

For the chanterelle cream

2 tablespoons unsalted butter

2 shallots, chopped

8 ounces chanterelle mushrooms,
    trimmed and sliced

5 tablespoons dry white wine

⅔ cup heavy cream

3 tablespoons chopped fresh chervil

2 tablespoons chopped fresh chives

For the hollandaise sauce

12 tablespoons (1½ sticks) unsalted butter

2 egg yolks

2 teaspoons lemon juice

salt and freshly ground black pepper

1 Roll out the pastry on a floured surface to form a rectangle 4 inches longer and 2 inches wider than the fillets. Trim into a fish shape, decorate with a cookie cutter to represent scales and glaze with beaten egg. Chill for 1 hour and then bake at 400°F for 30–35 minutes, until well risen and golden. Remove from the oven and split open horizontally. Reduce the oven temperature to 325°F.

2 To make the chanterelle cream, melt the butter and fry the shallots gently until soft but not colored. Add the mushrooms and cook until their juices begin to run. Pour in the wine, increase the heat and boil to evaporate the liquid. When dry, add the cream and herbs and bring to a simmer. Season well, transfer to a bowl, cover and keep warm.

3 Place the salmon in a fish kettle or roasting pan. Add the wine, carrot, onion, celery, thyme and enough water to cover. Slowly bring just to the boiling point, remove from the heat, cover and let the fish cook in this low heat for 30 minutes.

4 To make the sauce, melt the butter, skim the surface and pour into a bowl, leaving behind the milky residue. Place the egg yolks and 1 tablespoon of water in a glass bowl and place over a pan of simmering water. Whisk the yolks until thick and foamy. Remove from the heat and very slowly whisk in the butter. Add the lemon juice and season.

5 Place one salmon fillet on the base of the pastry, spread with the chanterelle cream and cover with the second fillet. Cover with the top of the pastry "fish" and warm through in the oven for 10–15 minutes. Garnish with kale and serve with the sauce.

Whole Cooked Salmon

Farmed salmon has made this fish more affordable and less of a treat, but a whole salmon still makes a great centerpiece at parties. It is never served with cold meats, but is usually accompanied by salads and mayonnaise. As with all fish, the taste depends on freshness and on not overcooking it, so although you need to start the preparation early, the cooking time is short.

INGREDIENTS

Serves about 10 as part of a buffet

1 fresh whole salmon, 5–6 pounds

2 tablespoons oil

1 lemon

salt and freshly ground black pepper

lemon wedges, cucumber and fresh dill
    sprigs, to garnish

1 Wash the salmon and dry it well, inside and out. Pour half the oil onto a large piece of strong foil and place the fish in the center.

2 Put a few slices of lemon inside the salmon and arrange some more on the top. Season well and sprinkle on the remaining oil. Wrap up the foil to make a loose parcel. Put the parcel on another sheet of foil or a baking sheet and bake at 400°F for 10 minutes. Turn off the oven, do not open the door and let sit for several hours.

3 To serve the same day, remove the foil and peel off the skin. If you are keeping it for the following day, leave the skin on and chill the fish overnight. Arrange the fish on a large platter and garnish with lemon wedges, cucumber cut into thin ribbons and sprigs of dill.

Baked Cod with Garlic Mayonnaise

This unusual way of preparing cod is adapted from an Italian recipe for more typical Mediterranean fish.

INGREDIENTS

Serves 4

4 anchovy fillets

3 tablespoons chopped fresh parsley

6 tablespoons olive oil

4 cod fillets, about 1½ pounds total, skinned

¼ cup bread crumbs

coarsely ground black pepper

For the garlic mayonnaise

2 garlic cloves, finely chopped

1 egg yolk

1 teaspoon Dijon mustard

¾ cup vegetable oil

salt and freshly ground black pepper

1 Make the mayonnaise. First put the garlic in a mortar or small bowl and mash it to a paste. Beat in the egg yolk and mustard. Add the oil in a continuous thin stream, while beating vigorously with a small wire whisk. When the mixture is thick and smooth, season with salt and pepper. Cover the bowl and keep cool.

2 Chop the anchovy fillets very finely with the parsley. Place in a small bowl and add pepper to taste and 3 tablespoons of the oil. Stir to a paste.

3 Place the cod fillets in a single layer in an oiled baking dish. Spread the anchovy paste on the top of the cod fillets. Sprinkle with the bread crumbs and the remaining oil. Bake at 400°F for 20–25 minutes or until the bread crumbs are golden. Serve hot with the garlic mayonnaise.

Monkfish Medallions with Thyme

Monkfish has a sweet flesh that combines particularly well with Mediterranean flavors.

INGREDIENTS

Serves 4

1¼ pounds monkfish fillet, preferably in a single piece

3 tablespoons extra virgin olive oil

½ cup small black olives, pitted

1 large or 2 small tomatoes, seeded and diced

1 fresh thyme sprig or 1 teaspoon dried thyme leaves

salt and freshly ground black pepper

1 tablespoon very finely chopped fresh parsley, to garnish

1 Remove the gray membrane from the monkfish, if necessary. Cut the fish into slices ½ inch thick.

2 Heat a non-stick frying pan until it is quite hot, without oil. Sear the fish quickly on both sides. Remove and set aside.

3 Pour 1 tablespoon of the olive oil in the base of a shallow baking dish and tilt to coat. Arrange the fish in a single layer. Scatter the olives and diced tomato on top of the fish.

4 Sprinkle the fish with thyme, salt and pepper and the remaining oil. Bake at 400°F for 10–12 minutes.

5 To serve, divide the medallions between 4 warmed plates. Spoon on the vegetables and any cooking juices. Sprinkle with the chopped parsley.

Breaded Fish with Tartar Sauce

All the taste of the classic fish dish but without any frying.

Serves 4

½ cup dried bread crumbs

1 teaspoon dried oregano

½ teaspoon cayenne pepper

1 cup milk

4 pieces of cod fillet, about 1½ pounds

3 tablespoons butter or margarine, melted

salt

For the tartar sauce

½ cup mayonnaise

½ teaspoon Dijon mustard

1–2 pickled gherkins, finely chopped

1 tablespoon drained capers, chopped

1 teaspoon chopped fresh parsley

1 teaspoon chopped fresh chives

1 teaspoon chopped fresh tarragon

salt and freshly ground black pepper

1 Grease a shallow ovenproof baking dish. Combine the bread crumbs, oregano and cayenne pepper on a plate and blend together. Mix the milk with 2 teaspoons salt in a bowl, stirring well to dissolve the salt.

2 Dip the pieces of cod fillet in the milk, then transfer to the plate and coat with the bread crumb mixture.

3 Arrange the coated fish in the prepared baking dish, in a single layer. Drizzle the melted butter over the fish.

4 Bake in the center of the oven at 450°F for 10–15 minutes, until the fish flakes easily when tested with a fork.

5 Meanwhile, combine all the ingredients for the tartar sauce in a small bowl. Stir gently to mix thoroughly. Serve the fish hot, accompanied by the tartar sauce, passed separately.

Smoked Haddock Lyonnaise

Lyonnaise dishes take their name from the city of Lyons, known for its excellent food. The term "Lyonnaise" refers to dishes prepared or garnished with onions.

INGREDIENTS

Serves 4

1 pound smoked haddock

⅔ cup milk

1 tablespoon butter

2 onions, chopped

1 tablespoon cornstarch

⅔ cup plain yogurt

1 teaspoon ground turmeric

1 teaspoon paprika

4 ounces mushrooms, sliced

2 celery stalks, chopped

2 tablespoons olive oil

12 ounces firm cooked potatoes, preferably cold, diced

1–2 ounces soft white bread crumbs

salt and freshly ground black pepper

flat leaf parsley, to garnish

2 Melt the butter and fry half the chopped onions until translucent. Stir in the cornstarch, then gradually blend in the fish cooking liquid and the yogurt and cook until thickened and smooth.

3 Stir in the turmeric, paprika, mushrooms and celery. Season to taste and add the flaked fish. Spoon into an ovenproof dish.

4 Heat the oil and fry the remaining onions until translucent. Add the diced potatoes and stir until lightly coated in oil. Sprinkle on the bread crumbs and seasoning.

5 Spoon this mixture over the fish and bake at 375°F for 20–30 minutes. Garnish with flat leaf parsley.

1 Put the smoked haddock and the milk into a large pan over low heat and poach the fish for about 15 minutes, until just cooked. Remove the haddock, reserving the cooking liquid, then flake the fish and discard the skin and any bones. Set aside.

Sand Dab Provençal

Recreate the taste of the Mediterranean with this easy-to-make fish dish.

Serves 4

4 large sand dab fillets

2 small red onions

½ cup vegetable stock

¼ cup dry red wine

1 garlic clove, crushed

2 zucchini, sliced

1 yellow bell pepper, seeded and sliced

1 can (14 ounces) chopped tomatoes

1 tablespoon chopped fresh thyme

salt and freshly ground black pepper

potato gratin, to serve (optional)

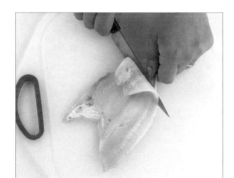

1 Skin the sand dab fillets with a sharp knife by laying them skin side down. Holding the tail end, push the knife between the skin and flesh in a sawing movement. Hold the knife at an angle with the blade angled toward the skin.

2 Cut each onion into 8 wedges. Put into a heavy saucepan, together with the stock. Cover and simmer for 5 minutes. Uncover and continue to cook, stirring occasionally, until the stock has reduced entirely. Add the wine and garlic clove to the pan and continue to cook until the onions are soft.

3 Add the zucchini, yellow pepper, tomatoes and thyme and season with salt and pepper to taste. Simmer for 3 minutes. Spoon the sauce into a large casserole.

4 Fold each fillet in half and place on top of the sauce. Cover and bake at 350°F for 15–20 minutes, until the fish is opaque and cooked. Serve immediately with potato gratin, if desired.

Stuffed Swordfish Rolls

Swordfish is abundant in the waters around Sicily and is featured in many dishes there.

Serves 4

4 slices fresh swordfish, about ½ inch thick

6 tablespoons olive oil

1 garlic clove, finely chopped (optional)

¼ cup bread crumbs

2 tablespoons capers, rinsed, drained and chopped

10 leaves fresh basil, chopped

¼ cup fresh lemon juice

salt and freshly ground black pepper

For the tomato sauce

2 tablespoons olive oil

1 garlic clove, crushed

1 small onion, finely chopped

1 pound tomatoes, skinned

½ cup dry white wine

salt and freshly ground black pepper

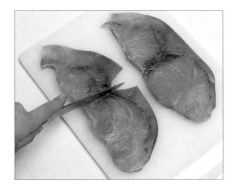

1 Cut the swordfish slices in half, removing any bones. Brush with 2 tablespoons of the olive oil, and refrigerate until needed.

2 Make the tomato sauce by heating the oil in a medium-size heavy saucepan. Add the garlic, and cook until golden. Discard the garlic. Add the onion, and cook over low heat until soft. Stir in the tomatoes and wine. Season with salt and pepper. Cover the pan, and cook over medium heat for 15 minutes.

3 Pass the sauce through a food mill or purée in a food processor. Keep warm while you prepare the fish.

4 In a small bowl combine 2 tablespoons of olive oil with the garlic, if using, bread crumbs, capers, basil and lemon juice. Season with salt and pepper and mix to a paste.

5 Lay the swordfish slices flat on a cutting board. Divide the stuffing mixture equally between the slices and spread it evenly over the center of each. Roll up the swordfish slices and secure with wooden toothpicks.

6 Heat the remaining oil in a flameproof dish. Add the swordfish rolls and brown them for 3–4 minutes over high heat, turning them once or twice. Pour in the tomato sauce and bake at 400°F for 15 minutes, basting occasionally. Serve warm.

Halibut with Fennel and Orange

The lovely sweet flavor of halibut can take strong accents like fennel and orange.

INGREDIENTS

Serves 4

4 tablespoons (½ stick) butter, plus extra
    for greasing
1 fennel bulb, thinly sliced
grated rind and juice of 1 orange
⅔ cup dry white wine
4 halibut steaks, about 7 ounces each
salt and freshly ground black pepper
fresh fennel fronds, to garnish

1 Butter a shallow baking dish and set aside. Add the fennel to a saucepan of boiling water, return to the boil and cook for 4–6 minutes, until just tender.

2 Meanwhile, put the orange rind, juice and wine in a small pan and boil until reduced by half.

3 Drain the fennel, then arrange in the baking dish and season. Arrange the halibut on the fennel, season, dot with butter, then pour on the reduced orange and wine.

4 Cover and bake at 350°F for about 20 minutes, until the flesh flakes. Serve immediately, garnished with fennel fronds.

Salmon with Cucumber Sauce

Cucumber and fresh dill are a perfect combination in this unusual hot sauce, which really complements the baked salmon.

INGREDIENTS

Serves 6–8

4 pounds salmon, gutted and scaled
melted butter, for brushing
3 parsley or thyme sprigs
½ lemon, halved
fresh dill sprigs, to garnish
orange slices and salad leaves, to serve

For the cucumber sauce

1 large cucumber, peeled
2 tablespoons butter
½ cup dry white wine
3 tablespoons finely chopped fresh dill
¼ cup sour cream
salt and freshly ground black pepper

1 Season the salmon and brush inside and out with melted butter. Place the herb sprigs and lemon in the cavity.

2 Wrap the salmon in foil, folding the edges together securely, then bake at 425°F for 15 minutes. Remove the fish from the oven and let sit in the foil for 1 hour, then remove the skin from the salmon.

3 Meanwhile, halve the cucumber lengthwise, scoop out the seeds, then dice the flesh.

4 Place the cucumber in a colander, toss lightly with salt and set aside for about 30 minutes to drain. Rinse well and pat dry.

5 Heat the butter in a small saucepan, add the cucumber and cook for about 2 minutes, until translucent but not soft. Add the wine to the pan and boil briskly until the cucumber is dry.

6 Stir the dill and sour cream into the cucumber and season to taste. Fillet the salmon and garnish with the fresh dill. Serve immediately with the cucumber sauce, orange slices and salad.

Sea Bass with Citrus Fruit

The sea bass family is found throughout most of the world's seas and is especially popular along the Mediterranean coast. Its delicate flavor is complemented by citrus fruits and fruity French olive oil.

INGREDIENTS

Serves 6

1 small grapefruit

1 orange

1 lemon

1 sea bass, about 3 pounds, cleaned
    and scaled

6 fresh basil sprigs

6 fresh dill sprigs

flour, for dusting

3 tablespoons olive oil

4–6 shallots, halved

¼ cup dry white wine

1 tablespoon butter

salt and freshly ground black pepper

1 Using a vegetable peeler, remove the rind from the grapefruit, orange and lemon. Cut into thin julienne strips, cover and set aside. Peel off the white pith from the fruits and, working over a bowl to catch the juices, cut out the segments from the grapefruit and orange and set aside for the garnish. Slice the lemon thickly.

2 Wipe the fish dry inside and out and season the cavity with salt and pepper. Make 3 diagonal slashes on each side. Reserve a few basil and dill sprigs for the garnish and fill the cavity with the remaining basil, dill, the lemon slices and half the julienne strips of citrus rind.

3 Dust the fish lightly with flour. In a roasting pan or flame-proof casserole large enough to hold the fish, heat 2 tablespoons of the olive oil over medium-high heat and cook the fish for about 1 minute, until the skin just crisps and browns on one side. Add the halved shallots.

4 Bake the fish at 375°F for about 15 minutes, then carefully turn the fish over and stir the shallots. Drizzle the fish with the remaining oil and bake for another 10–15 minutes, until the flesh is opaque throughout.

5 Carefully transfer the fish to a heated serving dish and remove and discard the cavity stuffing. Pour off any excess oil and add the wine and 2–3 tablespoons of the fruit juices to the pan. Bring to a boil over high heat, stirring. Add the remaining julienne strips of citrus rind and boil for 2–3 minutes, then whisk in the butter. Spoon the shallots and sauce around the fish, garnish with dill and the reserved basil and grapefruit and orange segments.

Sesame Baked Fish

Tropical fish are found increasingly at supermarkets, but Asian markets usually have a wider selection.

Serves 4–6

2 red snapper, parrot fish or monkfish
    tails, weighing about 12 ounces each

2 tablespoons vegetable oil

2 teaspoons sesame oil

2 tablespoons sesame seeds

1-inch piece fresh ginger, thinly sliced

2 garlic cloves, crushed

2 small fresh red chilies, seeded and
    finely chopped

4 shallots or 1 medium onion, halved
    and sliced

2 tablespoons water

½-inch square piece shrimp paste or
    1 tablespoon fish sauce

2 teaspoons superfine sugar

½ teaspoon cracked black pepper

juice of 2 limes

3–4 banana leaves or aluminum foil

lime wedges, to garnish (optional)

2 To make the marinade, heat the vegetable and sesame oils in a preheated wok, add the sesame seeds and fry until golden. Add the ginger, garlic, chilies and shallots and soften over low heat without burning. Add the water, shrimp paste or fish sauce, sugar, pepper, and lime juice. Bring to a boil and simmer for 2–3 minutes and set aside to cool.

3 If using banana leaves, remove and discard the central stem. Soften the leaves by dipping them in boiling water. To keep the leaves supple, rub all over with vegetable oil. Spread the marinade over the fish, wrap in the banana leaves and fasten with bamboo skewers, or wrap the fish in aluminum foil. Set the wrapped fish aside in a cool place for up to 3 hours to let the flavors mingle.

4 Place the wrapped fish on a baking sheet and bake at 350°F for 35–40 minutes. Alternatively, place on a wire rack and cook on a barbecue for 35–40 minutes. Garnish with lime wedges, if desired, and serve hot.

1 Clean the fish inside and out under cold running water. Pat dry with paper towels. Score both sides of each fish deeply with a knife to enable the marinade to penetrate effectively. If using parrot fish, rub with fine salt and let stand for 15 minutes. (This will remove the chalky coral flavor often associated with the parrot fish.)

Tahini Baked Fish

This dish is a favorite in many Middle Eastern countries, especially Egypt, Lebanon and Syria.

INGREDIENTS

Serves 6

6 cod or haddock fillets
juice of 2 lemons
¼ cup olive oil
2 large onions, chopped
1 cup tahini
1 garlic clove, crushed
3–4 tablespoons water
salt and freshly ground black pepper
rice and salad, to serve

1 Arrange the cod or haddock fillets in a large shallow casserole or baking dish. Pour over 1 tablespoon of the lemon juice and 1 tablespoon of the olive oil and bake at 350°F for about 20 minutes, or until the fish is cooked.

2 Meanwhile, heat the remaining oil in a large frying pan, and fry the onions for 6–8 minutes, until well browned and almost crisp.

3 Put the tahini and garlic in a small bowl and gradually beat in the remaining lemon juice and water, a little at a time, until the sauce is light and creamy. Season to taste with salt and pepper.

4 Sprinkle the onions on top of the fish and pour on the tahini sauce. Bake the fish for another 15 minutes, until the flesh is cooked through and the sauce is bubbling. Serve the fish immediately with rice and a salad.

Roast Monkfish with Garlic and Fennel

In the past, monkfish was often used as a substitute for lobster meat because it is very similar in texture. Today, it is appreciated in its own right and is delicious quickly roasted.

INGREDIENTS

Serves 4

2½ pounds monkfish tail

8 garlic cloves

1 tablespoon olive oil

2 bulbs fennel, sliced

juice of 1 lemon

1 bay leaf

salt and freshly ground black pepper

fresh bay leaves and finely grated lemon rind, to garnish

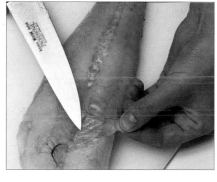

1 With a filleting knife, cut off the thin, transparent membrane covering the outside of the fish to prevent it from shrinking.

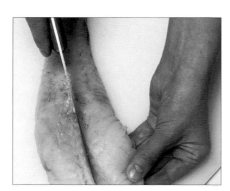

2 Cut along one side of the central bone to remove the fillet. Repeat on the other side.

3 Tie the two fillets together with string.

4 Peel and finely slice the garlic cloves and cut incisions into the fish flesh. Place the garlic slices into the incisions.

5 Heat the oil in a large, heavy saucepan and seal the fish on all sides.

6 Place the fish in a roasting pan, together with the fennel, lemon juice, bay leaf and seasoning. Roast at 425°F for about 20 minutes, until cooked through. Garnish with bay leaves and lemon rind, and serve immediately.

CASSEROLES
AND STEWS

Green Shrimp Curry

A popular, fragrant, creamy curry that takes very little time to prepare. It can also be made with thin strips of chicken meat.

INGREDIENTS

Serves 4–6

2 tablespoons vegetable oil

2 tablespoons green curry paste

1 pound raw jumbo shrimp, peeled and deveined

4 kaffir lime leaves, torn

1 lemon grass stalk, bruised and chopped

1 cup coconut milk

2 tablespoons fish sauce

½ cucumber, seeded and cut into thin batons

10–15 basil leaves

4 green chilies, sliced, to garnish

1 Heat the oil in a frying pan. Add the green curry paste and fry until bubbling and fragrant.

2 Add the shrimp, kaffir lime leaves and lemon grass. Fry for 1–2 minutes, until the shrimp have just turned pink.

3 Stir in the coconut milk and bring to a gentle boil. Simmer, stirring occasionally, for about 5 minutes or until the shrimp are tender. Do not overcook them.

4 Stir in the fish sauce, cucumber and basil, then top with the green chilies and serve.

Green Fish Curry

This dish combines all the typical flavors of the East.

INGREDIENTS

Serves 4

¼ teaspoon ground turmeric

2 tablespoons lime juice

4 cod fillets, skinned and cut into
    2-inch chunks

1 onion, chopped

1 fresh large green chili, roughly
    chopped

1 garlic clove, crushed

½ cup cashews

½ teaspoon fennel seeds

2 tablespoons dry shredded coconut

2 tablespoons oil

¼ teaspoon cumin seeds

¼ teaspoon ground coriander

¼ teaspoon ground cumin

⅔ cup water

¾ cup light cream or half-and-half

3 tablespoons finely chopped
    fresh cilantro

salt

fresh cilantro sprig, to garnish

vegetable pilaf, to serve (optional)

1 Combine the turmeric, lime juice and a pinch of salt and rub over the fish. Cover and let marinate for 15 minutes.

2 Meanwhile work the onion, chili, garlic, cashews, fennel seeds and coconut to a paste in a food processor or in a mortar with a pestle. Spoon the paste into a bowl and set aside.

3 Heat the oil in a large frying pan and fry the cumin seeds for 2 minutes, until they begin to splutter. Add the spice paste and fry for 5 minutes, then stir in the ground coriander, cumin and water. Fry, stirring frequently, for about 2–3 minutes.

4 Add the cream or half-and-half and the fresh cilantro. Simmer for 5 minutes. Add the fish and gently stir in. Cover and cook gently for 10 minutes, until the fish is tender. Garnish with a cilantro sprig and serve with vegetable pilaf, if desired.

Shrimp Curry with Quails' Eggs

Quails' eggs are available at specialty stores and delicatessens. Hens' eggs may be substituted if quails' eggs are hard to find. Use 1 hen's egg to every 4 quails' eggs.

INGREDIENTS

Serves 4

12 quails' eggs

2 tablespoons vegetable oil

4 shallots or 1 medium onion, finely chopped

1-inch piece fresh ginger, finely chopped

2 garlic cloves, crushed

2-inch piece lemon grass, finely shredded

1–2 small, fresh red chilies, seeded and finely chopped

½ teaspoon turmeric

½-inch-square piece shrimp paste or 1 tablespoon fish sauce

2 pounds raw shrimp, peeled and deveined

1⅔ cups canned coconut milk

1¼ cups chicken stock

4 ounces spinach, roughly shredded

2 teaspoons sugar

½ teaspoon salt

2 scallions, green part only, shredded, and 2 tablespoons dry shredded coconut, to garnish

2 Heat the vegetable oil in a large wok, add the shallots, ginger and garlic and soften without coloring. Add the lemon grass, chilies, turmeric and shrimp paste and fry briefly to bring out their flavors.

1 Cook the quails' eggs in boiling water for 8 minutes. Refresh in cold water, peel and then set aside.

3 Add the shrimp and fry briefly. Pour the coconut milk through a strainer over a bowl, then add the thin part of the milk with the chicken stock. Add the spinach, sugar and salt and bring to the boil. Simmer for 6–8 minutes.

4 Transfer to a serving dish, halve the quails' eggs and toss in the sauce. Scatter with the scallions and the shredded coconut and serve.

Parsi Shrimp Curry

This dish comes from the west coast of India, where fresh seafood is eaten in abundance. Fresh jumbo shrimp are ideal for this recipe.

INGREDIENTS

Serves 4–6

¼ cup vegetable oil

3 medium onions, 1 finely sliced and 2 finely chopped

6 garlic cloves, finely crushed

1 teaspoon chili powder

1½ teaspoons turmeric

¼ cup tamarind juice

1 teaspoon mint sauce

1 tablespoon brown sugar

1 pound raw jumbo shrimp, peeled and deveined

1 small bunch cilantro leaves, chopped

salt

fresh cilantro sprig, to garnish

1 Heat the oil in a frying pan and fry the sliced onion until golden brown. In a bowl, mix the garlic, chili powder and turmeric with a little water to form a paste. Add to the browned onion and simmer for 3 minutes.

2 Add the chopped onions and fry until they become translucent, then fold in the tamarind juice, mint sauce, sugar and salt. Simmer for another 3 minutes.

3 Pat the shrimp dry with paper towels. Add to the spice mixture with a small amount of water and stir-fry until the shrimp turn a bright orange-pink color.

4 When the shrimp are cooked, add the chopped cilantro leaves and stir-fry over high heat for a few minutes to thicken the sauce. Garnish with the cilantro and serve hot.

Pineapple Curry with Shrimp and Mussels

The delicate sweet-and-sour flavor of this curry comes from the pineapple, and although it seems an odd combination, it is absolutely delicious. Use the freshest shellfish that you can find.

INGREDIENTS

Serves 4–6

2½ cups coconut milk

2 tablespoons red curry paste

2 tablespoons fish sauce

1 tablespoon sugar

8 ounces raw jumbo shrimp, shelled and deveined

1 pound mussels, cleaned and "beards" removed

1½ cups fresh pineapple, finely crushed or chopped

5 kaffir lime leaves, torn

2 red chilies, chopped, and cilantro leaves, to garnish

1 Bring half the coconut milk to the boil and heat, stirring, until it separates.

2 Add the red curry paste and cook until fragrant. Add the fish sauce and sugar and continue to cook for a few moments.

3 Stir in the rest of the coconut milk and bring back to the boil. Add the jumbo shrimp, mussels, pineapple and kaffir lime leaves.

4 Reheat until boiling and then simmer for 3–5 minutes, until the shrimp are cooked and the mussels have opened. Remove any mussels that have not opened and discard. Serve immediately, garnished with chopped red chilies and coriander leaves.

Curried Shrimp in Coconut Milk

A curry-like dish in which shrimp are cooked in a spicy coconut gravy.

INGREDIENTS

Serves 4–6

2½ cups coconut milk

2 tablespoons yellow curry paste

1 tablespoon fish sauce

½ teaspoon salt

1 teaspoon sugar

1 pound raw jumbo shrimp, shelled and deveined

8 ounces cherry tomatoes

juice of ½ lime, to serve

red chili strips and cilantro, to garnish

1 Bring half the coconut milk to a boil. Add the yellow curry paste, stir until it disperses, then simmer for about 10 minutes.

2 Add the fish sauce, salt, sugar and remaining coconut milk. Simmer for another 5 minutes.

COOK'S TIP

To make yellow curry paste, process together 6–8 yellow chilies, 1 chopped lemongrass stalk, 4 shallots, 4 garlic cloves, 1 tablespoon chopped fresh ginger, 1 teaspoon coriander seeds, 1 teaspoon mustard powder, 1 teaspoon salt, ½ teaspoon ground cinnamon, 1 tablespoon light brown sugar and 2 tablespoons oil.

3 Add the shrimp and cherry tomatoes. Simmer very gently for about 5 minutes, until the shrimp are pink and tender.

4 Serve immediately, sprinkled with lime juice and garnished with chilies and cilantro.

Creole Fish Stew

A simple, attractive dish—good for an informal dinner party.

Serves 4–6

2 whole red bream or large snapper, cleaned and cut into 1-inch pieces
2 tablespoons seasoning salt
2 tablespoons malt vinegar
flour, for dusting
oil, for frying

For the sauce

2 tablespoons vegetable oil
1 tablespoon butter or margarine
1 onion, finely chopped
2 large fresh tomatoes, skinned and finely chopped
2 garlic cloves, crushed
2 thyme sprigs
2½ cups fish stock or water
½ teaspoon ground cinnamon
1 hot chili, chopped
1 red bell pepper, finely chopped
1 green bell pepper, finely chopped
salt
oregano sprigs, to garnish

1 Sprinkle the fish with the seasoning salt and malt vinegar, turning to coat. Set aside in the refrigerator to marinate for a minimum of 2 hours, or overnight.

2 When ready to cook, place a little flour on a large plate and coat the fish pieces, shaking off any excess flour.

3 Heat a little oil in a large frying pan and fry the fish pieces for about 5 minutes, until golden brown, then set aside. Do not worry if the fish is not cooked through; it will finish cooking in the sauce.

4 To make the sauce, heat the oil and butter in a large frying pan or wok and stir-fry the onion for 5 minutes. Add the tomatoes, garlic and thyme, stir well and simmer for another 5 minutes. Stir in the stock or water, cinnamon and hot chili.

5 Add the fish pieces and the chopped red and green bell peppers. Simmer until the fish is cooked through and the stock has reduced to a thick sauce. Adjust the seasoning with salt. Serve hot, garnished with oregano.

Indian Fish Stew

A spicy fish stew made with potatoes, peppers and traditional Indian spices.

INGREDIENTS

Serves 4

2 tablespoons oil

1 teaspoon cumin seeds

1 onion, chopped

1 red bell pepper, thinly sliced

1 garlic clove, crushed

2 red chilies, finely chopped

2 bay leaves

½ teaspoon salt

1 teaspoon ground cumin

1 teaspoon ground coriander

1 teaspoon chili powder

1 can (14 ounces) chopped tomatoes

2 large potatoes, cut into 1 inch chunks

1¼ cups fish stock

4 cod fillets

chappatis, to serve

1 Heat the oil in a large deep-sided frying pan and fry the cumin seeds for 2 minutes, until they begin to splutter. Add the onion, pepper, garlic, chilies and bay leaves and fry for 5–7 minutes, until the onions have browned.

2 Add the salt, ground cumin, ground coriander and chili powder and cook for 3–4 minutes.

3 Stir in the chopped tomatoes, potatoes and fish stock. Bring to a boil and simmer for another 10 minutes.

4 Add the fish, then cover and simmer for 10 minutes or until the fish is tender. Serve with freshly cooked chappatis.

Tanzanian Fish Curry

A deliciously fragrant sauce full of tender fish.

Serves 2–3

1 large snapper or red bream

1 lemon

3 tablespoons vegetable oil

1 onion, finely chopped

2 garlic cloves, crushed

3 tablespoons curry powder

1 can (14 ounces) chopped tomatoes

4 teaspoons smooth unsalted peanut
    butter

½ green bell pepper, chopped

2 slices fresh ginger

1 fresh green chili, seeded and
    finely chopped

2½ cups fish stock

1 tablespoon finely chopped fresh cilantro

salt and freshly ground black pepper

1 Season the fish, inside and out, with salt and pepper and place in a shallow bowl. Halve the lemon and squeeze the juice all over the fish. Cover loosely with plastic wrap and set aside to marinate for at least 2 hours.

2 Heat the oil in a large saucepan and fry the onion and garlic for 5–6 minutes, until soft. Reduce the heat, add the curry powder and cook, stirring constantly, for another 5 minutes.

3 Stir in the tomatoes and then the peanut butter, mixing well. Then add the green bell pepper, ginger, chili and stock. Stir well and simmer gently for 10 minutes.

4 Cut the fish into pieces and gently lower into the sauce. Simmer for another 20 minutes or until the fish is cooked. Using a slotted spoon, transfer the fish pieces to a plate.

5 Stir the cilantro into the sauce and adjust the seasoning. If the sauce is very thick, add a little extra stock or water. Return the fish to the sauce, cook gently to heat through and then serve immediately.

COOK'S TIP

The fish can be fried before it is added to the sauce, if preferred. Dip it in seasoned flour and fry in oil in a large frying pan or a wok for a few minutes before adding to the sauce.

Crab and Corn Gumbo

Gumbos are traditional Creole dishes, which come from New Orleans, Louisiana, and always contain a roux that gives this dish a distinctly rich flavor.

INGREDIENTS

Serves 4

2 tablespoons butter or margarine

2 tablespoons flour

1 tablespoon vegetable oil

1 onion, finely chopped

4 ounces okra, trimmed and chopped

2 garlic cloves, crushed

1 tablespoon finely chopped celery

2½ cups fish stock

⅔ cup sherry

1 tablespoon ketchup

½ teaspoon dried oregano

¼ teaspoon pumpkin pie spice

2 teaspoons Worcestershire sauce

2 corn cobs, sliced

1 pound crab claws

cayenne pepper

fresh cilantro sprigs, to garnish

1 Melt the butter or margarine in a large saucepan over a low heat, add the flour and stir together to make a roux. Cook for about 10 minutes, stirring constantly to prevent burning, while the roux turns golden brown and then darkens to a rich, nutty brown. If black specks appear, the roux must be discarded. Turn the roux onto a plate and set aside.

2 Heat the oil in the same saucepan over medium heat, add the onion, okra, garlic and celery and stir to combine. Cook for a few minutes, then add the fish stock, sherry, ketchup, oregano, pumpkin pie spice, Worcestershire sauce and cayenne pepper to taste.

3 Bring to a boil, then simmer gently for about 10 minutes, until the vegetables are tender. Add the roux, stirring it well into the sauce, and cook for a few minutes, until thickened.

4 Add the corn cobs and crab claws and continue to simmer gently over low heat for about 10 minutes, until the crab and corn are cooked.

5 Spoon onto warmed serving plates and garnish with sprigs of fresh cilantro.

Fisherman's Stew

A chunky, hearty stew that is warming in winter. The stock used here is especially aromatic, but if you do not have time to prepare it, use a basic fish stock instead.

INGREDIENTS

Serves 4

6 strips of bacon, cut into strips

1 tablespoon butter

1 large onion, chopped

1 garlic clove, finely chopped

2 tablespoons chopped fresh parsley

1 teaspoon fresh thyme leaves or
    ½ teaspoon dried thyme

1 pound tomatoes, skinned, seeded
    and chopped

⅔ cup dry vermouth or white wine

10 ounces potatoes, diced

1½–2 pounds skinless white fish fillets, cut
    into large chunks

salt and freshly ground black pepper

fresh flat leaf parsley sprig, to garnish

For the stock

8 ounces white fish trimmings, including
    heads and bones

2 tablespoons butter

1 shallot, finely chopped

1 leek, white part only, finely chopped

1 cup mushrooms, finely chopped

¼ cup dry white wine

2½ cups water

bouquet garni, consisting of 1 thyme
    sprig, 2 parsley sprigs and 1 bay leaf

small strip of dried orange peel

1 First make the stock. Put the fish trimmings in a large bowl, cover with cold water and set aside for 1–2 hours, then drain and chop into small pieces.

2 Melt the butter in a heavy saucepan, add the finely chopped shallot, leek and mushrooms and fry gently over low heat for 2–3 minutes, or until softened but not browned. Stir in the fish trimmings.

3 Add the wine and bring to a boil over high heat. Boil until reduced by half, then add the water and bring back to a boil. Skim the surface, add the bouquet garni and orange peel, lower the heat and simmer for 25 minutes. Strain the stock and set aside. Discard the vegetables, bouquet garni and orange peel.

4 Fry the bacon in a large saucepan over medium heat until lightly browned but not crisp, then remove the bacon and drain on paper towels.

5 Add the butter to the pan and gently fry the onion, stirring occasionally, for 3–5 minutes or until soft. Add the garlic, parsley and thyme and cook for 1 more minute, stirring constantly. Add the tomatoes, vermouth or white wine and the strained fish stock and bring to a boil.

6 Reduce the heat, cover and simmer the stew for about 15 minutes. Add the potatoes, cover again and simmer for another 10–12 minutes or until they are almost tender.

7 Add the chunks of fish and the bacon. Simmer gently, uncovered, for 5 minutes or until the fish is just cooked and the potatoes are tender. Adjust the seasoning, garnish with the flat leaf parsley and serve.

COOK'S TIP

It is worth taking the trouble to make fish stock. Fish trimmings are usually very cheap and sometimes even free, but do make sure that they are fresh. It is best to avoid oily fish, such as mackerel or sardines, but virtually all types of white fish are suitable. Remove any roe and gills before cooking, as these will make the stock bitter. Fish heads, in particular, yield the greatest flavor and nutritional content, and bones are also useful. Do not overlook the value of shrimp shells and heads, which, used on their own, make an aromatic and flavorful stock for poaching shellfish. They add a surprising amount of strength to a basic white fish stock, too. Try experimenting with different types of fish; there is surprising variation in the flavor and body produced. The preparation and cooking take little time, and it is worth bearing in mind that fish stock does not benefit from prolonged cooking, which will result in a bitter taste.

Seafood Stew

"Soups"—really stews—of mixed fish and shellfish are specialties of all Mediterranean countries.

INGREDIENTS

Serves 6–8

3 tablespoons olive oil

1 medium onion, sliced

1 carrot, sliced

½ stalk celery, sliced

2 garlic cloves, chopped

1 can (14 ounces) plum tomatoes, chopped, with their juice

4 cups water

8 ounces raw shrimp, shelled and deveined (reserve the shells)

1 pound white fish bones and heads, gills removed

1 bay leaf

1 sprig fresh thyme, or ¼ teaspoon dried thyme leaves

4 black peppercorns

1½ pounds fresh mussels, in their shells, scrubbed and rinsed

1 pound fresh small clams, in their shells, scrubbed and rinsed

1 cup white wine

2¼ pounds mixed fish fillets, such as cod, monkfish, red mullet or hake, cut into chunks

3 tablespoons finely chopped fresh parsley

salt and freshly ground black pepper

rounds of French bread, toasted, to serve

1 Heat the oil in a medium-size saucepan. Add the onion and cook slowly until soft but not colored. Stir in the carrot and celery and cook for another 5 minutes. Add the garlic, the tomatoes and their juice and 1 cup water. Cook over medium heat for about 15 minutes, until the vegetables are soft. Purée in a food processor or pass through a food mill. Set aside.

2 Place the shrimp shells in a large saucepan with the fish bones and heads. Add the herbs, peppercorns and remaining water. Bring to a boil, reduce the heat, and simmer for 25 minutes, skimming off any scum that rises to the surface. Strain and pour into a pan with the tomato sauce. Season to taste.

3 Place the mussels and clams in a saucepan with the wine. Cover and steam until all the shells have opened. Discard any that do not open.

4 Lift the mussels and clams out and set aside. Filter the cooking liquid through a layer of paper towels and add it to the stock and tomato sauce mixture. Check the seasoning.

5 Bring the sauce to a boil. Add the fish and boil for 5 minutes. Stir in the mussels and clams and cook for another 2–3 minutes. Transfer the stew to a warmed casserole. Sprinkle with parsley, and serve with the toasted rounds of French bread.

Italian Fish Stew

Italians are renowned for enjoying good food, especially if it is shared with all the members of an extended family. This stew is a veritable feast of fish and seafood in a delicious tomato broth, suitable for a more modest family lunch.

INGREDIENTS

Serves 4

2 tablespoons olive oil

1 onion, thinly sliced

a few saffron threads

1 teaspoon dried thyme

large pinch of cayenne pepper

2 garlic cloves, finely chopped

2 cans (14 ounces each) peeled tomatoes, drained and chopped

¾ cup dry white wine

8 cups hot fish stock

12 ounces skinless white fish fillets, cut into pieces

1 pound monkfish, membrane removed, cut into pieces

1 pound mussels in the shell, scrubbed and "beards" removed

8 ounces small squid, cleaned and cut into rings

2 tablespoons chopped fresh basil or parsley

salt and freshly ground black pepper

thickly sliced bread, to serve

1 Heat the oil in a large heavy saucepan. Add the onion, saffron, thyme, cayenne pepper and salt, to taste. Stir well and cook over low heat for 8–10 minutes, until the onion is soft. Add the garlic and cook for another minute.

2 Stir in the tomatoes, wine and fish stock. Bring to a boil and boil for 1 minute, then reduce the heat and simmer gently for 15 minutes.

3 Add the white fish fillet and monkfish pieces to the pan and simmer gently over low heat for another 3 minutes.

4 Add the mussels and squid rings and simmer for about 2 minutes, until the mussels open. Discard any that remain closed. Stir in the basil or parsley and season to taste. Ladle into warmed soup bowls and serve with bread.

Ragoût of Shellfish with Sweet Scented Basil

Green curry paste is an integral part of Thai cooking and can be used to accompany other dishes made with fish or chicken. Curry pastes will keep for up to 3 weeks stored in an airtight container in the refrigerator.

INGREDIENTS

Serves 4–6

1 pound fresh mussels in their shells, scrubbed and with "beards" removed

¼ cup water

8 ounces medium squid

1⅔ cups canned coconut milk

1¼ cups chicken or vegetable stock

12 ounces monkfish, hoki or red snapper, skinned

5 ounces raw or cooked shrimp, peeled and deveined

4 scallops, sliced (optional)

4 ounces green beans, trimmed and cooked

¼ cup canned bamboo shoots, drained

1 ripe tomato, skinned, seeded, and roughly chopped

4 sprigs large-leaf basil, torn, and strips of fresh red chili, to garnish

rice, to serve (optional)

For the green curry paste

2 teaspoons coriander seeds

½ teaspoon caraway or cumin seeds

3–4 fresh green chilies, finely chopped

4 teaspoons superfine sugar

3-inch piece lemon grass

¾-in piece ginger, finely chopped

3 garlic cloves, crushed

4 shallots or 1 medium onion, finely chopped

¾-inch-square piece shrimp paste

1 cup cilantro leaves, finely chopped

3 tablespoons fresh mint or basil, finely chopped

½ teaspoon ground nutmeg

2 tablespoons vegetable oil

salt

1 Place the mussels in a large saucepan, add the water, cover and cook for 6–8 minutes, until the shells open. Take three-quarters of the mussels out of their shells and set aside. (Discard any that have not opened.) Strain the cooking liquid and set aside.

2 To prepare the squid, trim off the tentacles beneath the eye. Rinse under cold running water, discarding the gut. Remove the "quill" from inside the body and rub off the paper-thin skin. Cut the body open and score with a sharp knife. Cut into strips and set aside.

3 To make the green curry paste, dry-fry the coriander and caraway seeds in a wok to release their flavor. Grind the chilies with the sugar and 2 teaspoons salt in a mortar with a pestle or in a food processor to make a smooth paste. Combine the seeds from the wok with the chilies, add the lemon grass, ginger, garlic and shallots, then grind or process until smooth.

4 Add the shrimp paste, cilantro, mint or basil, nutmeg and vegetable oil to the food processor or mortar. Combine well.

5 Pour the coconut milk into a strainer. Pour the thin part of the milk, together with the chicken stock and the reserved mussel cooking liquid, into a wok. Reserve the coconut milk solids. Add 4–5 tablespoons of the green curry paste, according to taste. You can add more paste later, if you need to. Boil rapidly until the liquid has reduced completely.

6 Add the coconut milk solids, then add the squid and monkfish. Simmer for 15–20 minutes. Then add the shrimp, scallops and cooked mussels with the beans, bamboo shoots and tomato. Simmer for 2–3 minutes, transfer to a bowl and decorate with the basil and chilies. Serve with rice, if desired.

Haddock and Broccoli Stew

This is an easy, one-pot meal full of color and texture.

INGREDIENTS

Serves 4

4 scallions, sliced

1 pound new potatoes, diced

1¼ cups fish stock or water

1¼ cups milk

1 bay leaf

½ bunch broccoli florets, sliced

1 pound smoked haddock fillets, skinned

1 can (7 ounces) corn, drained

freshly ground black pepper

chopped scallions, to garnish

crusty bread, to serve

1 Place the scallions and potatoes in a large saucepan and add the stock or water, milk and bay leaf. Bring the mixture to a boil, then cover the pan and simmer for 10 minutes.

2 Add the broccoli to the pan. Cut the fish into bite-size chunks and add to the pan with the corn.

3 Season the stew well with freshly ground black pepper, then cover the pan and simmer for another 5 minutes or until the fish is cooked through. Remove the bay leaf and transfer to a serving dish. Scatter on the scallions and serve hot with crusty bread.

COOK'S TIP

When new potatoes are not available, old ones can be used, but choose a waxy variety that will not disintegrate.

Hoki Balls in Tomato Sauce

This quick meal is a good choice for young children, as you can guarantee no bones. Its low fat content also makes it an ideal dish for anyone on a low-fat or low-cholesterol diet. If desired, add a dash of chili sauce.

INGREDIENTS

Serves 4

1 pound hoki or other white fish
   fillets, skinned

¼ cup fresh whole wheat bread crumbs

2 tablespoons snipped chives or scallions

1 can (14 ounces) chopped tomatoes

2 ounces button mushrooms, sliced

salt and freshly ground black pepper

fresh chives, to garnish

1 Cut the fish fillets into large chunks and place in a food processor. Add the whole wheat bread crumbs and the chives or scallions. Season to taste with salt and pepper and process until the fish is finely chopped, but still has some texture left.

COOK'S TIP
~

Hoki is a good choice for this dish, but if it is not available, use cod, haddock or whiting instead.

2 Divide the fish mixture into about 16 even-size pieces, then mold them into balls with your hands.

3 Place the tomatoes and mushrooms in a large saucepan and cook over medium heat until boiling. Carefully add the fish balls, cover and simmer for about 10 minutes, until cooked. Serve hot, garnished with chives.

Fish Stew with Calvados, Parsley and Dill

This rustic stew harbors all sorts of interesting flavors and will please and intrigue. Many varieties of fish can be used, just choose the freshest and best.

INGREDIENTS

Serves 4

2¼ pounds assorted white fish

1 tablespoon chopped fresh parsley, plus a
  few leaves to garnish

8 ounces mushrooms

1 can (8 ounces) tomatoes

1 large bunch fresh dill sprigs

2 teaspoons flour

1 tablespoon butter

2 cups cider

3 tablespoons Calvados

salt and freshly ground black pepper

1 Chop the fish roughly and place it in a casserole or stewing pot with the parsley, mushrooms, tomatoes and salt and pepper to taste. Reserve 4 dill sprigs to garnish and chop the remainder. Add the chopped dill to the casserole.

2 Work the flour into the butter with a fork. Heat the cider and stir into the flour and butter mixture with a spoon, a little at a time. Cook, stirring, until it has thickened slightly.

3 Add the cider mixture and the Calvados to the fish and mix gently. Cover and bake at 350°F for about 30 minutes or until cooked through. Serve immediately, garnished with reserved sprigs of dill and the parsley leaves.

Coconut Salmon

This is an ideal dish to serve at dinner parties.

Serves 4

2 teaspoons ground cumin

2 teaspoons chili powder

½ teaspoon ground turmeric

2 tablespoons white wine vinegar

4 salmon steaks, about 6 ounces each

3 tablespoons oil

1 onion, chopped

2 fresh green chilies, seeded and chopped

2 garlic cloves, crushed

1-inch piece fresh ginger, grated

1 teaspoon ground coriander

¾ cup coconut milk

salt

fresh cilantro sprigs, to garnish

scallion rice, to serve

1 Combine 1 teaspoon of the ground cumin with the chili powder, turmeric, vinegar and ¼ teaspoon salt. Rub the paste over the salmon steaks and let marinate for about 15 minutes.

2 Heat the oil in a large deep frying pan and fry the onion, chilies, garlic and ginger for 5–6 minutes. Put into a food processor or blender and process to a paste.

3 Return the paste to the pan. Add the remaining cumin, the coriander and coconut milk. Bring to a boil, lower the heat and simmer for 5 minutes.

4 Add the salmon. Cover and cook for 15 minutes, until the fish is tender. Transfer to a serving dish and garnish with cilantro. Serve with scallion rice.

COOK'S TIP

If coconut milk is unavailable, dissolve some grated creamed coconut in boiling water and strain into a bowl.

Moroccan Fish Tagine

Tagine is actually the name of the large Moroccan cooking pot used for this type of cooking, but you can use an ordinary casserole instead.

INGREDIENTS

Serves 4

2 garlic cloves, crushed

2 tablespoons ground cumin

2 tablespoons paprika

1 small fresh red chili (optional)

2 tablespoons tomato paste

¼ cup lemon juice

4 whiting or cod cutlets, about
    6 ounces each

4 tomatoes, sliced

2 green bell peppers, seeded and sliced

salt and freshly ground black pepper

chopped fresh cilantro, to garnish

steamed broccoli, to serve

1 Combine the garlic, cumin, paprika, chili, if using, tomato paste and lemon juice. Spread this mixture over the fish, then cover and chill for about 30 minutes to let the flavor penetrate.

COOK'S TIP

If you are preparing this dish for a dinner party, it can be assembled completely and stored in the refrigerator, ready to bake when needed.

2 Arrange half the tomatoes and half the green peppers in a baking dish. Season with salt and pepper to taste.

3 Cover with the fish, in a single layer, then arrange the remaining tomatoes and green peppers on top. Cover the baking dish with foil and bake at 400°F for about 45 minutes. Garnish with chopped cilantro and serve with steamed broccoli.

Octopus and Red Wine Stew

Unless you are happy to clean and prepare octopus for this Greek dish, buy one that is ready for cooking.

INGREDIENTS

Serves 4

2 pounds prepared octopus

1 pound onions, sliced

2 bay leaves

4 ripe tomatoes

¼ cup olive oil

4 garlic cloves, crushed

1 teaspoon superfine sugar

1 tablespoon chopped fresh oregano
    or rosemary

2 tablespoons chopped fresh parsley

⅔ cup red wine

2 tablespoons red wine vinegar

chopped fresh herbs, to garnish

warm bread and pine nuts, to serve

1 Put the octopus in a saucepan of gently simmering water with one-quarter of the sliced onions and the bay leaves. Cook gently for 1 hour.

2 While the octopus is cooking, plunge the tomatoes into boiling water for 30 seconds, then refresh in cold water. Peel off the skins and chop roughly.

3 Drain the octopus and, using a sharp knife, cut it into bite-size pieces. Discard the sliced onions and bay leaves.

4 Heat the oil in a saucepan and fry the octopus, the remaining chopped onions and the crushed garlic for 3 minutes. Add the tomatoes, sugar, oregano or rosemary, parsley, wine and vinegar and cook, stirring constantly, for 5 minutes, until the mixture is pulpy.

5 Cover the pan and cook over the lowest possible heat for 1½ hours, until the sauce is thickened and the octopus is tender. Garnish with fresh herbs and serve with plenty of warm bread and pine nuts to scatter over the top.

Index